Books are to be returned on or before
the last date below

100 IDEAS THAT
CHANGED THE WEB

You can and must understand computers NOW.

COMPUTER

LIB

100 IDEAS THAT CHANGED THE WEB

Jim Boulton

Laurence King Publishing

Introduction

The last 20 years has seen the birth and rise of the Web at an astronomical pace. We have witnessed the birth of the Information Age, equal in magnitude to the transition to the modern world from the Middle Ages. We do everything differently. Just as Gutenberg's printing press allowed the accumulated knowledge of the human race to reach every person who could read, the Web extends this knowledge to everyone with access to a computer.

This book is meant to be an accessible introduction to the history of the Web, but we would not have the Web if it were not for the internet. In fact, we don't get to the invention of the World Wide Web until idea 21, the preceding ideas lay its foundations. So this is not only a book of ideas that changed the Web, it also includes those that led to its creation.

While there is a lot of cross-referencing in the book, each essay stands alone. Much as Tim Berners-Lee envisaged the Web, the reader can dip in and out of the book at will, following the links between ideas or reading chronologically from beginning to end. The choice is yours.

Our story starts and ends with a dream. In 1934, a Belgian bibliophile dreamt of a telescope that could transmit electronic documents. In 1999, Tim Berners-Lee outlined his vision for a Semantic Web. An information space of an unimaginable amount of data, automatically interrogated, processed and turned into knowledge. A dream that is now within our grasp.

In between, we have 98 other ideas. Some are revolutionary, like the peer-to-peer network. Others are humble, like the GIF. All of them have contributed to the world-changing phenomenon that is the World Wide Web.

Ideas 1–20 examine the precursors, those ideas that led to the creation of the Web. Without hypertext, the modem, the Graphical User Interface, the mouse, the PC and of course the internet,

there would be no Web. The Web and the internet are terms that are often erroneously interchanged, before we get any further, perhaps now is a good time to clarify the difference. The internet is a global system of interconnected computer networks. It is the infrastructure that carries email, instant messaging, Voice over IP, network games, file transfer and the Web. The Web is the most accessible component of the internet, an interlinked system of hypertext documents.

Ideas 21–53 deal with the Web's infancy, introducing the browser, the JPEG, search, multi-player gaming, the webcam, the banner ad, net art, webmail and the blog. These early years were a time of experimentation, a DIY landscape typified by the now-deleted GeoCities. It was a rich period of creative expression dominated by nonconformists. Hackers, artists, and other misfits dived into the unknown and changed the world. Tragically, evidence of this culturally significant period is largely lost. The story of the first webpage, published in August 1991, is typical. It was continually overwritten until March 1992. No copy of the original webpage, not even a screenshot, exists.

Ideas 54–71 address the pre-social Web and the birth of ecommerce. At the end of the last century, dot-com hysteria was in full force. Broadband arrived and the Web began to lose its original spirit. Brands entered cyberspace, as it was then known. Websites became more polished, recognizing the commercial demands of their paymasters. The pivotal moment was the appearance of digital wallets, primarily PayPal. There was a reaction: John Perry Barlow, member of The Grateful Dead, declared 'the Independence of Cyberspace' and Shawn Fanning created the first peer-to-peer network. He called it Napster. Then came the crash: those companies that survived not only had deep pockets, they had user-generated content at their heart. Amazon had customer reviews, eBay had user-driven auctions, Wikipedia was entirely written and edited by its users. Even Google had user-generated links.

With ideas 74–98, the Web came of age, becoming dynamic, social and, crucially, mobile. In the early years of the Web, pages were built entirely in HTML. With each click, a new page was loaded. Even a small change to the page meant the entire page had to be refreshed. In 2005, Google launched Google Maps, which behaved more like a software application than a website. Web 2.0 had arrived and with it came the social Web. Although sites like Blogger and Friendster had started long beforehand, it was in 2006 that the social Web really took off. That year, Facebook opened up to everyone of 13 and older, Twitter was founded, YouTube went mainstream, and aggregators like Fark suddenly had the power to take servers down. The launch of the iPhone in 2007 took the Web mobile, at least in Europe and the US, by this point the number of people in Asia accessing the Web via mobile phone exceeded the number browsing on a PC. Our most important device became the one in our pocket. It's the one screen that cuts across our work and leisure time. It's the first screen we look at in the morning and the last one we look at at night.

With ideas 99 and 100 we look to the future. When the Web was first conceived, it was intended to be more than an interconnected library of information. The ultimate aim was a system that drew meaning from this information. In an increasingly connected world, our ability to capture and store data is staggering. When this data is marked up with contextual information, it becomes knowledge and we are one step closer to a Web that thinks. The Semantic Web.

With only 100 ideas, there is not room for every innovation that shaped the Web. The Mother of all Demos, Social Bookmarks, Bitcoin, Twitch TV and the Hash Tag were incorporated within other ideas, others were dismissed entirely. Sorry Shockwave, we had some good times together but it was never going to last. As for the Active Desktop, you were interesting but in the end, just too demanding. The less said about Chat Roulette the better. It was for research purposes, honestly.

While writing this book, it became apparent that exploring the history of the Web is not just a nostalgic trip into our recent digital past but an exploration of the very way we think and communicate. Our thought processes are non-linear and erratic but the way we make sense of things and express ourselves is linear. Pioneers like Paul Otlet, Vannevar Bush, Theodor Nelson, Douglas Engelbart and Tim Berners-Lee questioned this conviction. Their legacy is the World Wide Web. A place that breaks down national and cultural borders. A place that blurs the boundaries between generating and exchanging ideas. A place that has toppled regimes and created new economic models. A place that has radically changed the way we work, play, shop, socialize and otherwise participate in society. But above all, a place that is for everyone.

The idea of the internet was born in Belgium

IDEA № 1

THE MUNDANEUM

In 1934, six decades before the birth of the Web, a Belgian bibliophile described his vision for a *télé photographie*, an electronic telescope which could transmit any document in the world to a television screen.

Paul Otlet, founder of the Mundaneum and creator of the Universal Decimal Classification system.

Paul Otlet loved libraries. In 1891 he met a kindred spirit, fellow Belgian and future Nobel Prize winner, Henri La Fontaine. Together they conceived the Mundaneum, a comprehensive collection of the world's published knowledge, equal in ambition to the great Library of Alexandria.

By 1910, they had collected thousands of books, newspapers, photographs, journals, posters and postcards. Otlet called the collection the Réseau, a network of documents connected by 'links' detailed on index cards. More than blind signposts, these links indicated the relationships between documents, an implementation of what we now call the **Semantic Web**. As the Mundaneum grew, this degree of annotation became unmanageable. Otlet put his mind to new technologies that would overcome the limitations of paper-based records. In his 1935 book *Monde*, he describes 'a machinery unaffected by distance which would combine at the same time radio, X-rays, cinema and microscopic photography.... From afar anyone would be able to read any passage that would be projected onto his individual screen, thus in his armchair, anyone would be able to contemplate the whole of creation or particular parts of it.'

Otlet described the Web six decades ahead of its invention, even predicting social networks with remarkable accuracy, expecting users to 'participate, applaud, give ovations and sing in the chorus'. A true visionary, Otlet also foresaw the mobile revolution, writing in 1906, 'Tomorrow, telephony will be wireless ... Everyone will carry, in his or her pocket, a tiny little handset that will be tuned with the turn of a screw to the wavelength adopted by each emitting centre.'

Otlet died in 1944 with his life's work in ruins, destroyed to make way for an exhibition of Third Reich art. Following the war, he was almost forgotten as American pioneers such as Vannevar Bush, Douglas Engelbart and Theodor (Ted) Nelson came to the foreground. It was not until W. Boyd Rayward published Otlet's biography in 1975 that the remarkable prescience of his work became apparent.

The Mundaneum museum opened in Mons, Belgium, in 1998, and in 2012, Google offered its support, recognizing Paul Otlet and Henri La Fontaine as its spiritual forefathers. Vinton Cerf, inventor of the internet, says it as it is: 'The idea of the internet was born in Belgium.' ■

'A true visionary, Otlet also foresaw the mobile revolution.'

Volunteers at the Mundaneum classified around 17 million publications. Their work has become known as the Index Card Internet.

Creating an indestructible network

IDEA № 2
THE SPACE RACE

Donald Davies (left) and Paul Baran (right), the inventors of packet switching, the defining technology of the internet.

On 4 October 1957, the Soviet Union launched the first man-made satellite into space, *Sputnik I*. Its pride hurt, the US poured billions of dollars into scientific research. One of the side-effects was the birth of the internet.

Following World War II, the US formed the RAND Corporation to continue the innovative spirit that had produced radar and the atomic bomb. RAND's first project was the production of an artificial satellite. Unbeknown to them, the Soviet Union was ahead of the game and achieved the huge propaganda coup first. The US vowed never to be humiliated in such a way again, eventually putting a man on the moon in the ultimate display of one-upmanship.

Key to winning the space race was the establishment of ARPA, the Advanced Research Projects Agency, the first director of which was Joseph Licklider. Not only did Licklider want to put a man on the moon, but also he wanted to create an Intergalactic Computer Network. It was 1958. Over at RAND, Paul Baran was tasked with designing a communications system that could survive a nuclear attack. These two projects would later come together to create the internet.

Baran's design for an indestructible communications system was counter to the established norms of telephony. Rather than being based on an end-to-end chain of connections – a relay – Baran proposed dividing messages into blocks, sending them via multiple paths and reassembling them on arrival. In the UK, Welsh computer scientist Donald Davies drew the same conclusion. He called his solution 'packet switching'. Davies and Baran learned of each other's work and decided to collaborate.

Meanwhile, Bob Taylor, Licklider's successor at ARPA, was funding three computer projects – an air-defence system, a computer time-sharing project and an operating system. He had a console for each in his office, all of which did pretty much the same thing. Combining all three projects seemed logical, and packet switching looked to be the solution.

BBN Technologies got the job, and on 29 October 1969 they successfully connected computers at the University of California (Los Angeles) and the Stanford Research Institute. Within a month, nodes at the University of California (Santa Barbara) and the University of Utah had been added. Known as ARPANET, this was the world's first packet-switching network and the first step towards the Intergalactic Computer Network, which we now know as the internet. ∎

One small step for man, one giant leap for network communications.

The birth of non-linear narratives

HYPERTEXT

Screen-based text with embedded links to other text has revolutionized how we find and retrieve information. Yet until the mid-twentieth century, conditioned by 500 years of print, non-linear narratives were unimaginable to most.

Vannevar Bush, author of 'As We May Think', which describes The Memex (Memory-Index), a proto-hypertext system.

The rapid advancements in knowledge brought about by World War II were disorientating. Organizing and acting on the deluge of opportunities that suddenly presented themselves was beyond linear narratives and taxonomies. A cognitive leap was required.

Vannevar Bush, Director of the Manhattan Project and the brain behind the atomic bomb, was disillusioned by man's pursuit of power rather than progress. He put his mind to discovering how the world's knowledge could be harnessed instead for the common good. The result was his seminal essay 'As We May Think', first published in the *Atlantic* in 1945. In it, he described the Memex, a device that could store and index every book and record created.

A collective memory machine was not a revolutionary idea; H. G. Wells had expressed similar ideas in his collection of essays 'World Brain'. Bush's ideas had more in common with those of Argentine novelist Jorge Luis Borges, whose 1941 spy story 'The Garden of Forking Paths' was perhaps the first multilinear narrative. What was radical about the Memex was that it mimicked the human mind, which 'operates by association. With one item in its grasp, it snaps instantly to the next … in accordance with some intricate web of trails carried by the cells of the brain.'

As World War II played out its end game, a young radar technician based in the Philippines came across 'As We May Think' in an old copy of the *Atlantic*. His name was Douglas Engelbart. He saw the Memex as an evolved radar, with ranks of operators analysing,

'The brain behind the atomic bomb was disillusioned by man's pursuit of power rather than progress.'

processing and linking information. After the war Engelbart became Director of the Augmentation Research Center at Stanford Research Institute – a position he retained for almost 20 years – and in 1962 he introduced his 'oNLine System' (NLS), the first practical implementation of Bush's ideas (see **Graphical User Interface**).

Around the same time, a Harvard student called Theodor (Ted) Nelson envisioned a 'docuverse', an information space where text was liberated from paper. He had imagined the World Wide Web 30 years before its invention. Nelson named his project Xanadu, after Coleridge's opium-induced poem; perhaps appropriately it remains a pipe dream (see **Xanadu**). Nelson went on to coin the term 'hypertext', and predicted the personal computer revolution. Although Xanadu has never been realized, Nelson's ideas have influenced every hypertext system since. ∎

After his involvement in the creation of the atomic bomb, Vannevar Bush turned his efforts towards ways of sharing scientific understanding for the positive advancement of mankind.

Get off the internet,
I need to make a call

IDEA № 4

THE MODEM

The modem is the digital descendant of the telegraph, enabling computers to send data to each other over a telephone line. Short for 'modulator-demodulator', it translates an analogue signal into a digital signal, and vice-versa. Before the modem made it possible to visit other people's machines, the computer was simply a useful tool. The modem turned it into a place.

An ad for the Hayes Smartmodem, offering fast download speeds of 1.2k per second.

Until 1968, AT&T had a monopoly on the use of its phone lines, only allowing its own Bell Laboratories devices to be connected to its network. This led to the emergence of acoustically coupled modems that were clumsily connected to a phone through its handset. Even after 1968, rules for electronically coupling a device to phone lines were complex. Only large corporations could afford the required computer-driven modems.

Working at one of these corporations was computer hobbyist Dennis Hayes. Exposed to computerized modems every day, he saw no reason why one could not be made for the Altair 8800 he had at home. He set about designing a prototype and gathered the parts. In 1977, on his dining-room table, together with his friend Dale Heatherington, Hayes built the first PC modem. At $49.95 for the unassembled bare board, the catchily

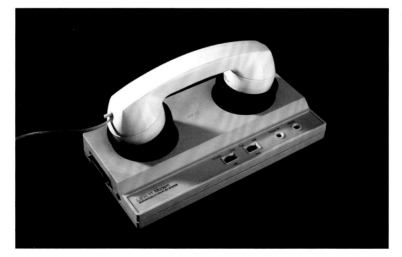

An Anderson Jacobson ADC 300 baud acoustic-coupler modem.

> 'Before the modem made it possible to visit other people's machines, the computer was simply a tool. The modem turned it into a place.'

SMARTMODEM

Hayes

AA   CD   OH   RD   SD   R   MR

named 80-103A proved extremely popular with Altair owners. Hayes and Heatherington quit their jobs at National Data Corporation and formed D.C. Hayes Associates. They had created a new industry.

Sales improved with their next model, the Micromodem 100, and further still when they added the Micromodem II for the Apple II, but a different device for each machine meant business was tough. Hayes and Heatherington needed a one-size-fits-all solution, which meant a programmable, rather than a hardwired, device. But how would the device distinguish between instruction and data? The solution was for the modem to operate in two modes. In data mode, information was forwarded as normal. In command mode, information was instead interpreted as commands. Known as the Hayes command set, the modem would start up in command mode and change to data mode after receiving three plus signs (+++) followed by a one-second pause. The Hayes Smartmodem was released in July 1981, the first modem that could be used with any computer.

The launch of the World Wide Web in 1991 increased demand for dial-up modems exponentially. This growth, fuelled by the very modems invented by Hayes, proved their downfall. Hayes Microcomputer Products, as they were now called, could not keep pace with the rapid transition from 14k to 56k modems. Saddled with mountains of redundant stock, they went out of business in 1999.

When **broadband** technology was introduced at the turn of the century, routers, network switches, WiFi and modems were combined in a single device. Within this device, Hayes and Heatherington's legacy lives on. ∎

The Hayes Smartmodem, released in 1981, the first universal modem. The Hayes command set remains the basis for controlling most modems to this day.

'While most computer scientists focused on making *computers* smarter, Engelbart was interested in how computers could make *humans* smarter. '

Ivan Sutherland's Sketchpad (1963) was the first program to utilize a graphical user interface. Using an X-Y Plot display and light pen, it also pioneered object-orientated programming.

IDEA № 5

GRAPHICAL USER INTERFACE

At the 1968 Joint Computer Conference – a live demonstration that has since become known as the 'Mother of All Demos' – Douglas Engelbart demonstrated his vision for the future of computing. It was the graphical user interface (GUI).

Inspired by the work of Vannevar Bush and Ivan Sutherland, Engelbart's oNLine System (NLS) was the first implementation of a GUI, a virtual desktop incorporating windows, menus, icons and folders. For an industry used to dealing with punch cards and command lines, this was radical thinking. While most computer scientists were focusing on making *computers* smarter, Engelbart was interested in how computers could make *humans* smarter.

Several of Engelbart's team went on to develop the groundbreaking Xerox Alto. However, it would not be Xerox that steered the course of modern computing. After a visit to Xerox PARC, the research centre established to design the future of computing, Steve Jobs saw the GUI first hand. In 1983, Apple released the Lisa, the first home computer with a GUI and mouse. Much to Apple's irritation, Microsoft quickly followed suit, releasing Windows 1.0 the same year. Steve Jobs accused Bill Gates of plagiarism, Gates countered, 'Well, Steve, I think it's more like we both had this rich neighbour named

Xerox and I broke into his house to steal the TV set, to find out that you had already stolen it.'

America Online (see p.28) knew a good idea when they saw one and adopted the GUI in 1989, opening up the internet beyond the technical community. History repeated itself with the Web. Like the PC and the internet before it, it was when Mosaic released the first point-and-click **browser** that the Web started to appeal to a wider audience. It was 1993.

Mosaic evolved into Netscape Navigator, launching with the slogan 'The Web is for everyone'. Microsoft saw this was true and released its Internet Explorer browser, copying most of Netscape's functionality. Twenty years on, Internet Explorer, Firefox, Safari and most browsers since remain remarkably similar to Netscape's original model. Some see this as a missed opportunity; others see it as testament to Engelbart's thinking 25 years earlier. What everyone agrees on is that without the GUI, the Web would not be the global phenomenon it is today. ∎

Of mice and men

IDEA № 6
THE MOUSE

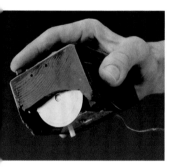

The first computer mouse, held by its inventor, Douglas Engelbart (1963).

Despite the rapid development of computer technology over the last 50 years, the design of the computer mouse has remained more or less unchanged. Even with the advent of touchscreen technology, this classic product looks set to retain its position as the input device of choice for some time yet.

The precursor of the mouse – the trackball – was invented by the Canadian Navy in 1952. It consisted of a five-pin bowling ball mounted in a bracket that tracked which way the ball was turned. The mouse also has a naval connection. While working as a radar operator in the Philippines at the end of World War II, Douglas Engelbart began to explore how screen-based technology could help solve complex problems. He envisioned people sitting in front of displays, using computers to formulate and organize their ideas efficiently.

After the war, as Director of the Augmentation Research Center (ARC) at Stanford Research Institute, Engelbart led a team that designed and developed the oNLine System (NLS), a human–computer interface that incorporated hypertext, the graphical user interface (GUI) and the first computer mouse.

Developed in 1963 by Engelbart and Bill English, the mouse was the device that made **hypertext** feasible. Without it, there would be no hyperlink, and without the hyperlink there would be no Web. For a joke, Engelbart and English nicknamed this world-changing device the 'mouse', as the lead attached to the rear of the device looked like a tail. The name stuck. Several other pointing devices were developed by Engelbart's team, including light pens, joysticks and head-mounted devices, but ultimately the mouse proved the most effective. The GUI and the mouse were publically demonstrated at the 1968 Joint Computer Conference (see **Graphical User Interface**).

In 1968, the German company Telefunken took the best elements of the trackball and Engelbart's mouse, and created the roller-ball mouse, or Rollkugel. The design is so successful

'Without the mouse, there would be no hyperlink, and without the hyperlink there would be no Web.'

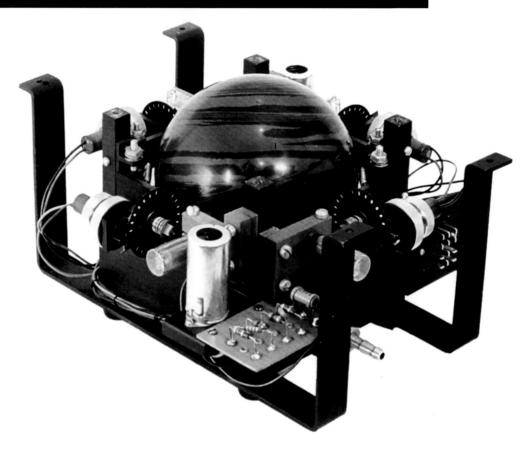

that, despite advances in technology, a roller-ball mouse can still be bought today.

Bill English went on to work for Xerox PARC, and the mouse became the key component of the revolutionary Xerox Alto computer system and its 1981 follow-up, the Xerox Star. The Xerox Star's mouse was the first to be available on the commercial market, although at $75,000 for a basic system, take-up was low. It was not until 1983, when Apple released the Apple Lisa for a more accessible $10,000, that the mouse was recognized as an essential part of home computing. ∎

The precursor of the mouse, the trackball (1952), was developed by the Canadian Navy and used a standard Canadian five-pin bowling ball.

'Markup language evolved from the marking up of paper manuscripts by editors.'

The computerized descendant of typesetting

IDEA № 7
MARKUP LANGUAGE

HTML is to the Web what moveable type is to the printing press. As moveable type allows printers to typeset their publications, HTML allows web developers to design a web page. Without it, there would be no Web.

The first computer mark-up language, RUNOFF, was created in 1964 by Jerome Saltzer for MIT's time-sharing system. Inspired by RUNOFF, William Tunnicliffe created a version that worked across different operating systems. Originally called GenCode, it evolved into Standard Generalized Markup Language (SGML).

With the rise of WYSIWYG (what you see is what you get) software at the end of the 80s, it looked like the end of markup language. Nothing could be further from the truth. In 1991, Tim Berners-Lee created the first webpage using a derivative of SGML. He called it Hypertext Markup Language (HTML).

One of the core technologies of the Web, HTML consists of 'tags' within a web page that format text, indicate links and embed objects. Tags usually have an opening <BOLD> and closing tag </BOLD>. A web browser reads these tags and composes the webpage according to their instructions. Based on only 18 basic instructions, the simplicity of HTML was a major factor in the proliferation of the Web.

During the **browser** wars of the mid-90s, different versions of HTML emerged, causing inconsistencies in the way webpages were displayed. To address this, in 1996 Berners-Lee created the World Wide Web Consortium (W3C), which has maintained HTML specifications ever since.

Another markup language widely used on the Web is XML (eXtensible Markup Language). Also developed and maintained by W3C, its purpose is to introduce flexibility, allowing developers to create any tags they need. The main difference between HTML and XML is that HTML is designed to be read by a browser whereas XML is designed to be read by an application of the developer's choice.

The fifth version of HTML – HTML5 – has been under development since 2007. It adds in-built support for many of the multimedia features required by today's web users, including audio, video and scaleable vector graphics, avoiding the need for proprietary plug-ins such as Flash. A stable version of HTML5 is due for release by the end of 2014. ∎

When type was set by hand, a small number of 'galley proofs' would be printed for markup by the editor and/or the author. On receipt of the edits, the printer would adjust the type, and print final copies.

'Down with Cybercrud!'

IDEA № 8

XANADU

Dream Machines *explores the creative potential of networked computers and introduced the world to* hypertext. *Nelson calls his vision Xanadu, a multimedia docuverse of interconnected flying pages.*

In 1974, Theodor Nelson released a two-part book *Computer Lib/ Dream Machines*. In it, he predicted the home-computer revolution and the World Wide Web.

Computer Lib is a call to arms. With the rallying cry 'Down with Cybercrud' it demands that ordinary people rise up and claim computers for themselves. The second half of the book, *Dream Machines*, describes the unlimited potential of branching media and networked content. Nelson called his vision Xanadu.

In Nelson's Xanadu, text is liberated from paper. A journey through this 'docuverse' is controlled by a virtual throttle. As the reader accelerates through the text, gaps appear between words and sentences, which are instantly populated by new words and phrases, which Nelson calls 'transclusions'. Pulled from other documents, these transclusions add an ever-increasing amount of detail and background information. Push back on the throttle and detail is omitted, while the writing becomes more concise.

Nelson describes Xanadu as a different kind of computer world, based on a different kind of electronic document; he talks of flying pages, deep interconnection and parallel intercomparison. However, his central insight is that content remains separate from structure. Instead of packaging everything into a single file, the page pulls the content point from its source.

Xanadu has never been fully realized but it has inspired every hypertext system since – notably Apple's pioneering hypermedia software, HyperCard, and Tim Berners-Lee's World Wide Web. Nelson is unimpressed by both. The graphical metaphor of HyperCard falls into what he calls a 'virtual reality trap'. Instead of challenging the print metaphor, **HyperCard** simulates it. He is equally damning of the Web, dismissing it as a gross over-simplification of Xanadu. In his words, 'HTML is precisely what we were trying to prevent, ever-breaking links, links going outward only, quotes you can't follow to their origins, no version management, no rights management.'

Nelson is supposedly responsible for more entries in the *Oxford English Dictionary* than Lewis Carroll. More tellingly, he conceived many of the ideas we now take for granted. Yet Nelson's key achievement is greater still: he changed our understanding of what a computer was for and who could use it. ∎

You can and must understand computers NOW.

COMPUTER

LIB

Computer Lib/Dream Machines
*was the first book about the personal
computer, telling ordinary people
'You can and must understand
computers NOW'.*

SEVEN DOLLARS.

First Edition.

Time *magazine 'Person of the Year', 1981*

An IBM Personal Computer running MS-DOS.

IDEA № 9

THE PERSONAL COMPUTER

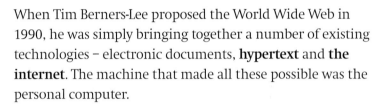

When Tim Berners-Lee proposed the World Wide Web in 1990, he was simply bringing together a number of existing technologies – electronic documents, **hypertext** and **the internet**. The machine that made all these possible was the personal computer.

In 1971, a two-year-old electronics company called Intel was commissioned to produce an integrated circuit for a groundbreaking new product, the electronic calculator. The challenge was to create an inexpensive microchip, small enough to fit inside a pocket-sized device. Intel employee number 12, Ted Hoff, led the project. Instead of hardwiring the logic into the circuit, he designed a programmable chip. He had created the microprocessor, a chip that could be programmed to perform the operations of a calculator, or anything else for that matter. The world would never be the same again.

In Albuquerque, New Mexico, Ed Roberts was running a company called Micro Instrumentation and Telemetry Systems (MITS) that sold kits for these new-fangled pocket calculators. By 1975, pre-built devices were hitting the market at ever-lower prices and the company was struggling. Roberts decided to try to do what few had attempted – to create a home-assembly kit for a computer. *Popular Electronics* magazine heard about his idea and were keen to feature it on the cover. Roberts had not made the computer yet

– it did not even have a name – but he did have an impressive blue case with lots of lights and switches. *Popular Electronics* published a picture of the empty case on its front cover. An ad in the magazine marketed the Altair, named after a planet on *Star Trek*, for $397. MITS received thousands of orders. Roberts needed a working machine fast. He hired two Harvard students to write an operating system. Those students were Paul Allen and Bill Gates. Six weeks later they had created Disk Operating System (DOS). Roberts had created the computer that would spark the digital revolution.

The next year, in 1976, a group of computer hobbyists in the San Francisco Bay area organized the Homebrew Computer Club. One of the members was Steve Wozniak, then aged 24. He had designed a much more sophisticated machine than the Altair, with a monitor and a keyboard. He shared his designs at the club and asked for advice. Steve Jobs gave him some: 'Don't give your ideas away for free.' The pair formed Apple, marketing Wozniak's computer as the Apple I.

'By 1980, over a million people owned a home computer.'

Companies like Atari, Commodore, Sinclair and Texas Instruments joined the market, and by 1980 over a million people owned a microcomputer. IBM took note. They built their own model assembled from off-the-shelf parts. They called it the IBM Personal Computer. All they needed was an operating system. They tracked down a couple of former Harvard students in New Mexico that were rumoured to have one. By now Allen and Gates had formed Microsoft; they licensed DOS – now called MS-DOS – to IBM for a per-unit fee. Less than four months after the launch, *Time* magazine named the IBM PC 'Person of the Year'.

It did not take long for competitors to see that the IBM PC was made from components they could buy at their local electronics store. Copycats began to build identical machines in their basements, also licensing MS-DOS from Microsoft. Two of these copycats were Compaq and Dell. The battle between Apple machines and IBM clones commenced. Soon every home and office would have one or the other. It was not long before someone had the smart idea of connecting them all up. ∎

The Xerox Alto (1973) was the first true personal computer, incorporating a keyboard, monitor, GUI and **mouse**, *but it was never sold commercially.*

'When the day came, the main emotion was relief. There were no grand celebrations... With hindsight, it's obvious it was a momentous occasion.'

The location of every IP address on the internet, as visualized by the Opte Project.

The infrastructure that carries the Web

IDEA № 10
THE INTERNET

The terms 'World Wide Web' and 'internet' are often used interchangeably, which is plain wrong. The internet is a global system of interconnected computer networks. It is the infrastructure that carries email, instant messaging, Voiceover IP, network games, file transfer and, of course, the Web.

The origins of the internet reach back to ARPANET, the communications system designed by the US government to survive a nuclear attack (see **The Space Race**). Paul Baran's solution was to divide messages into packets, send them via multiple paths and reassemble them on arrival – a system that became known as packet switching. The first message was sent over ARPANET on 29 October 1969. Charley Kline attempted to log into the Stanford network from the University of California. The system crashed as he reached G, but the letters L and O had been successfully sent.

By 1971, ARPANET incorporated nodes all over the US, and other countries were also developing their own packet-switching networks. Donald Davies, the co-inventor of packet switching, had built Mark I at the National Physical Laboratory in the UK. Norway had developed NORSAR. France had launched Cyclades. But all these packet-switching networks had different rules and so could not talk to one another. Robert Kahn and Vinton Cerf decided to establish a common protocol, which would become Transfer Control Protocol/Internet Protocol (see **Internet Protocol Suite**).

In November 1977, a successful test was conducted between networks in the US, the UK and Norway. It worked. All packet-switching networks were urged to migrate to the new protocol and eventually a deadline of 1 January 1983 was given.

Vinton Cerf recalls, 'When the day came, the main emotion was relief. There were no grand celebrations – I can't even find a photograph. Yet, with hindsight, it's obvious it was a momentous occasion. On that day, the operational internet was born.'

Computer scientists, engineers and academics had already adopted packet-switching networks. Suddenly, they could talk to one another across networks. They were able to share files, send email, chat and play simple games. **Internet service providers** (ISPs) and **bulletin board systems** (BBSs) appeared, games got more sophisticated and online communities developed. All the ingredients existed for the global phenomenon that the internet has become today, bar one. You still needed to be technically minded to access the Net. Everything changed on 6 August 1991 when Tim Berners-Lee launched the first webpage. Suddenly the internet could be used by anyone. ■

Open versus closed networks

INTERNET SERVICE PROVIDER

An internet service provider (ISP) provides access to the internet in the same way that a telephone company provides access to a telephone network.

In the late '90s, half of all the CDs produced worldwide had an AOL logo on them, and the company was acquiring a new subscriber every six seconds.

After building ARPANET, the first packet-switching network (see **The Space Race**), BBN Technologies set out to create a private-sector equivalent. In 1975, it launched Telenet. Various organizations paid monthly fees to connect to it, allowing them to send email, chat, share files and access **bulletin board systems**.

In 1979, computer time-sharing business CompuServe began offering a dial-up information service to consumers. Sold through Radio Shack stores, the service proved more popular than anyone anticipated. People signed up to access news and use email, but the big attraction was CompuServe's 'CB Simulator' chat software (see **Web Chat**).

CompuServe's first serious competitor, an online service for Commodore 64 owners, launched in 1985. Q-Link offered a raft of services aimed at a less technical audience, including an interactive adventure game called Habitat, one of the first **'massively multiplayer' games**, capable of supporting large numbers of participants. In 1989, Q-Link extended its service to IBM-compatible PCs and changed its name to America Online. With its user-friendly interface, low monthly fee and aggressive marketing it quickly became the dominant ISP.

As the Web grew, the 'walled garden' of restricted services offered by ISPs like CompuServe and AOL became less appealing. A number of new ISPs emerged, offering unrestricted access to the Web. In 1994, Prodigy became the first of the early-generation dial-up services to offer full access. AOL and CompuServe stubbornly stuck to their guns and slowly lost market share, AOL acquiring CompuServe in 1997.

AOL finally relented in 2006. It looked as though unrestricted access to a free, open internet was the Web's only future. This turned out not to be the case. To the horror of many, the most successful online businesses today – the Apple Store, Amazon Kindle and Facebook – all operate closed networks.

Has the walled garden won out or will history repeat itself? Initially, users like the comfort of a stable, easy-to-understand platform. Networks need the reassurance a monopoly gives them to grow. As users get more sophisticated, this becomes less satisfactory. People become less willing to put up with the restrictions, and an innovative new entrant to the market comes along with a fresh approach. Perhaps, like AOL and CompuServe before them, Facebook and Apple's closed-network approach will ultimately be their undoing. ∎

Compuserve was the first and largest Internet Service Provider in the US. AOL stole its dominant position by offering internet access for a flat monthly subscription rather than charging by the hour.

LAST NIGHT WE EXCHANGED LETTERS WITH MOM, THEN HAD A PARTY FOR ELEVEN PEOPLE IN NINE DIFFERENT STATES AND ONLY HAD TO WASH ONE GLASS...

That's CompuServe, The Personal Communications Network For Every Computer Owner

And it doesn't matter what kind of computer you own. You'll use CompuServe's Electronic Mail system (we call it Email™) to compose, edit and send letters to friends or business associates. The system delivers any number of messages to other users anywhere in North America.

CompuServe's multi-channel CB simulator brings distant friends together and gets new friendships started. You can even use a scrambler if you have a secret you don't want to share. Special interest groups meet regularly to trade information on hardware, software and hobbies from photography to cooking and you can sell, swap and post personal notices on the bulletin board.

There's all this and much more on the CompuServe Information Service. All you need is a computer, a modem,

and CompuServe. CompuServe connects with almost any type or brand of personal computer or terminal and many communicating word processors. To receive an illustrated guide to CompuServe and learn how you can subscribe, contact or call:

CompuServe

Information Service Division, P.O. Box 20212
5000 Arlington Centre Blvd., Columbus, OH 43220
800-848-8990
In Ohio call 614-457-8650

An H&R Block Company

Circle 98 on inquiry card.

```
/\\\\\\\\\\\        /\\\\\\\\\\\        /\\\\\\\\\\\
\/\\\///////\\\     \/\\\///////\\\     /\\\///////\\\
 \/\\\      \/\\\   \/\\\      \/\\\    \/\\\     \///
  \/\\\\\\\\\\\\/    \/\\\\\\\\\\\\/     \///\\\
   \/\\\///////\\\   \/\\\///////\\\      \///\\\
    \/\\\      \/\\\  \/\\\      \/\\\        \///\\\
     \/\\\      \/\\\  \/\\\      \/\\\  /\\\    \//\\\
      \/\\\\\\\\\\\\/   \/\\\\\\\\\\\\/  \///\\\\\\\\\\\/
       \////////////    \////////////    \/////////
```

The Mundaneum ...	[01]	ISP ...	[11]
The Space Race ...	[02]	Bulletin Boards ...	[12]
Hypertext ...	[03]	Hackers ...	[13]
The Modem ...	[04]	Cyberpunk	[14]
The GUI ...	[05]	Internet Protocol ...	[15]
The Mouse ...	[06]	Desktop Publishing ...	[16]
Markup Language ...	[07]	Hypercard ...	[17]
Xanadu ...	[08]	The GIF ...	[18]
The PC ...	[09]	Emoticon ...	[19]
The Internet ...	[10]	Domain Names ...	[20]

Press [C] to continue _

A potential design for a 100 Ideas that Changed the Web *bulletin board system.*

Antisocial phreaks get social

IDEA № 12
BULLETIN BOARD SYSTEMS

WHOLE EARTH CATALOG

access to tools

Spring 1969
$4

The WELL, an acronym for 'Whole Earth 'Lectronic Link', was the Bulletin Board of the Whole Earth Catalog (shown above). A regular meeting place for fans of the Grateful Dead, it was where John Perry Barlow, John Gilmore and Mitch Kapor met, founders of the Electronic Frontier Foundation (see **The Independence of Cyberspace***).*

Twenty years before the Web and 30 years before Facebook, an antisocial hacker put his computer on **the internet** and invited people to visit. He had created the first computerized bulletin board system (BBS).

Ward Christensen created the first BBS during a blizzard in January 1978. Snowed in, he called his friend Randy Suess with an idea to create the online equivalent of a cork notice board. Randy suggested they keep it simple: 'Just the two of us – you do the software, I'll do the hardware. When will the software be ready?'

Two weeks later was the answer, but they told everyone a month, thinking it sounded more believable. The system was simple. Only one person could be connected at a time. And all they could do was leave a message, or upload or download a file. Christensen and Suess announced their creation in the November 1978 issue of *Byte* magazine. Within a year, they had more than 10,000 users.

Clones of their system sprang up around the world. The first generation of boards attracted hackers, gamers and amateur radio enthusiasts. Before long, there were boards for everyone, perhaps the most famous being The WELL, short for Whole Earth 'Lectronic Link, a countercultural BBS popular with fans of the Grateful Dead.

To avoid long-distance charges, most users visited local boards, but some had other ideas. They became 'phreakers' – phone freaks who hacked the telephone system to avoid these expenses. Legendary phreaker John Draper discovered that the free whistles given out in Cap'n Crunch cereal boxes produced a 2600-hertz tone, the same tone AT&T used to signal a free internal call. A long whistle reset the line, short whistles dialled numbers – one blast for a '1', two blasts for a '2', etc. More ambitious phreakers used pliers and crocodile clips to hook up directly to the network.

Bulletin board systems reached their peak usage in the mid-90s, when the Web took off. Some of the larger commercial BBSs, like The WELL, evolved into **internet service providers**. The rest faded away, but their legacy is undisputed. Bulletin board systems were the first social networks. Ironically, they were inhabited by the antisocial, and it was their subversive rants and dreams that shaped today's online world. ∎

Steal this network!

IDEA Nº 13
HACKERS

Abbie Hoffman's Steal This Book *exemplifies '60s counterculture and the hacker ethic.*

The use of the term 'hacker' to mean someone who exploits weaknesses in a computer system is controversial. In computer subculture, it is a badge of honour, meaning someone with an advanced understanding of computers.

Hackers are fundamentally nerds, young engineers who play with a technology, manipulating and transforming it until it becomes transparent. Nerds invented the Web and many other technologies we now take for granted. Traditionally, young entrepreneurs are respected by society. However, during the '70s the nerd developed a subversive streak. This rebellious attitude was a spin-off of the hippie movement of the '60s, and one of its leading figures was Abbie Hoffman.

Hoffman encouraged people to 'drop out' of society and to scam the system. As the corporate structure was financing the Vietnam War, it was a political duty to dodge your subway fare and avoid paying for utilities. In *Steal this Book*, he describes a number of methods to enable agitators to do just that. The hacker ethic had been born.

Hacking stories became folklore during the '80s. In the 1983 film *War Games*, the protagonist hacks into a remote military computer and almost causes World War III. This kind of hysteria was not reserved for movies either. Possibly the most infamous real-life hacker was serial offender Kevin Mitnick. He was branded Public Enemy No.1 by the FBI. When he was eventually

caught, he was given six years in prison, some of which was in solitary confinement because it was believed he could 'start a nuclear war by whistling into a pay phone'. Notoriously, on 2 November 1988, Robert Tappan Morris wrote a self-replicating, self-propagating program known as the Internet Worm. His aim, he claims, was to measure the size of the internet. It crippled thousands of computers within a matter of hours, confirming everyone's worst fears about what a hacker could do. Morris was sentenced to three years' probation for what essentially was a prank gone wrong.

More recent hacks have been of a political nature. Anonymous is a loose coalition of hacktivists that began with a protest at attempts to suppress anti-Scientology content on the Web. It has since developed into a broader movement against online censorship. It has carried out denial-of-service attacks and other protests against anti-piracy organizations, child pornography sites, and corporations including PayPal and Sony. Anons were early supporters of the global Occupy movement and the Arab Spring. In 2012, *Time* magazine called Anonymous one of the '100 most influential people' in the world.

Matthew Broderick and Ally Sheedy in the 1983 film War Games.

'The myth of the hacker masks their contribution to digital culture.'

The myth of the hacker masks the contribution they have made. From a very early stage in the growth of the internet, volunteer programmers donated their time, energy and creativity to help to improve it for everyone. The hacker ethos is responsible for the internet, the PC, bulletin boards, open-source software, the Web and countless other applications that make the internet what it is today. ∎

Wanted poster for Kevin Mitnick, a serial hacker who first gained unauthorized access to a computer network at the age of 16.

U.S. Department of Justice
United States Marshals Service

WANTED
BY U.S. MARSHALS

NOTICE TO ARRESTING AGENCY: Before arrest, validate warrant through National Crime Information Center (NCIC).

United States Marshals Service NCIC entry number: (NIC/ _V721460021_).

NAME: ....MITNICK, KEVIN DAVID

AKS (S): ....MITNIK, KEVIN DAVID
MERRILL, BRIAN ALLEN

DESCRIPTION:

Sex:.........................MALE
Race:........................WHITE
Place of Birth:..............VAN NUYS, CALIFORNIA
Date(s) of Birth:............08/06/63; 10/18/70
Height:......................5'11"
Weight:......................190
Eyes:........................BLUE
Hair:........................BROWN
Skintone:....................LIGHT
Scars, Marks, Tattoos:.......NONE KNOWN
Social Security Number (s): ..550-39-5495
NCIC Fingerprint Classification: ...DOPK20PM13DIPM199M09

ADDRESS AND LOCALE: KNOWN TO RESIDE IN THE SAN FERNANDO VALLEY AREA OF CALIFORNIA AND
LAS VEGAS, NEVADA

WANTED FOR: VIOLATION OF SUPERVISED RELEASE
ORIGINAL CHARGES: POSSESSION UNAUTHORIZED ACCESS DEVICE; COMPUTER FRAUD
Warrant Issued: CENTRAL DISTRICT OF CALIFORNIA
Warrant Number: 9312-1112-0154-C

DATE WARRANT ISSUED: NOVEMBER 10, 1992

MISCELLANEOUS INFORMATION: SUBJECT SUFFERS FROM A WEIGHT PROBLEM AND MAY HAVE EXPERIENCED
WEIGHT GAIN OR WEIGHT LOSS
VEHICLE/TAG INFORMATION: NONE KNOWN OFTEN USES PUBLIC TRANSPORTATION

If arrested or whereabouts known, notify the local United States Marshals Office, (Telephone: _213-894-2485_).

If no answer, call United States Marshals Service Communications Center in McLean Virginia.
Telephone (800)336-0102: (24 hour telephone contact) NLETS access code is VAUSMOOOO.

Form USM -132
(Rev. 3/2/92)

PRIOR EDITIONS ARE OBSOLETE AND NOT TO BE USED

November 1992

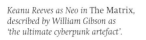

Keanu Reeves as Neo in The Matrix, *described by William Gibson as 'the ultimate cyberpunk artefact'.*

The future is already here –
it's just not very evenly distributed

IDEA № 14
CYBERPUNK

William Gibson's groundbreaking debut novel *Neuromancer*, published in 1984, was the first novel to win a clean sweep of the Hugo, Nebula and Philip K. Dick science-fiction awards. It heralded a new genre in sci-fi – cyberpunk – repainting the computer nerd as a hard-boiled anti-hero.

Set in the near future, cyberpunk describes an information-age dystopia where organized crime, drug addiction and corruption are rife. Mega-corporations have replaced governments as centres of political, economic and military power. Technology is ubiquitous and body modification is the norm. The prototype character is a lone hacker, permanently jacked into an artificially intelligent computer network – cyberspace.

In *Neuromancer*, the narrator explains, 'The matrix has its roots in primitive arcade games ... Cyberspace. A consensual hallucination experienced daily by billions ... a graphic representation of data abstracted from banks of every computer in the human system.' Overtly inspired by Jean Baudrillard's concept of Simulacra and Simulations, cyberpunk is a critique of postmodern culture. It suggests that we live in a simulated world, where images and signs have replaced reality, producing a hyper-reality. This illusion turns us into docile consumers, distracted from the ills of society. Cyberpunk writers like Gibson, Bruce Sterling and Neal Stephenson forcibly wake us from our daydream and encourage us to question the status quo.

With its embittered heroes and deadly *femmes fatales*, cyberpunk is a clear descendant of noir, but it also owes a debt to the beatniks. Just as Kerouac's *On the Road* was inspired by the Interstate Highway, Gibson's *Neuromancer* was inspired by the information superhighway. As the beatniks anticipated the hippie movement, cyberpunk anticipated digital counterculture.

Computer networks, the Web, augmented reality and artificial intelligence are all cyberpunk staples – the genre gives us a language to explore and extend these phenomena as they emerge. Without Cyberpunk we would not have cyberspace, avatars, megastructures, nanotech, wetware or Whuffie. As William Gibson says, 'The future is already here, it's just not very evenly distributed.' ∎

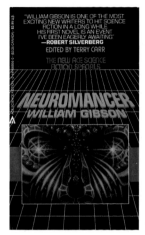

First-edition paperback cover, Ace Books 1984.

The rules of information exchange

IDEA № 15

INTERNET PROTOCOL SUITE

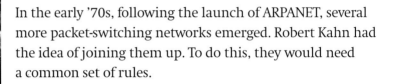

In the early '70s, following the launch of ARPANET, several more packet-switching networks emerged. Robert Kahn had the idea of joining them up. To do this, they would need a common set of rules.

Researchers from the Stanford Research Institute monitor the first Internet transmission, taking place in the garden of the Alpine Inn.

One of these networks was a packet radio system that operated out of a converted bread van provided by Stanford Research Institute (SRI). A regular stop was the Alpine Inn. Known locally as Zott's, it was described in 1909 by the president of SRI as 'unusually vile, even for a roadhouse, a great injury to the University and a disgrace to San Mateo County'. This view was not shared by Stanford students.

It was outside Zott's, on 22 November 1977, that the van sent a message to London via Norway and back to California by satellite. It travelled 90,000 miles in two seconds. At that moment, outside a biker bar in Silicon Valley, the internet was born.

This first successful test used Transmission Control Protocol (TCP), but as the Net grew, more protocols were required. User Datagram Protocol (UDP) was created for files where speed was more important than sequence, such as voice and game play. Internet Protocol (IP) was developed at a higher level to label and transport packets. This suite of protocols became known as TCP/IP. Its evolution over the next 20 years was managed by one of the driving forces of the internet, Jon Postel.

In 1982, the decision was made to convert all networks on ARPANET to TCP/IP by the end of the year. On 1 January 1983 the switch was made permanent and barely celebrated. With hindsight we realize what a momentous occasion this was. (see **The Internet**) It heralded the start of the Information Age.

By the late '80s, most public networks had joined the internet, but commercial traffic was banned from the government-sponsored platform. In 1988, Vinton Cerf asked to connect one commercial system, MCI Mail, as a test. As he anticipated, when the other email providers found out, they clambered to join too. They all ran on TCP/IP. Once they were on the internet, all these previously isolated networks could talk to one another. Kahn's vision had been realized.

Kahn and Cerf get the glory but, like most things, the success of TCP/IP is down to many people. Chief among them perhaps is Postel. The behaviour he encouraged, known as Postel's Law, seems wise beyond the implementation of TCP/IP: 'Be conservative in what you do, be liberal in what you accept from others.' ∎

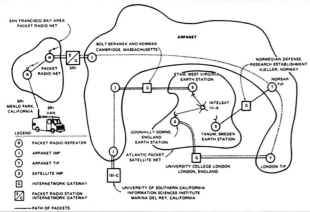

The inside of the converted bread van from which the first message was sent over the internet.

'Be conservative in what you do, be
liberal in what you accept from others.'

The self-publishing revolution

IDEA № 16

DESKTOP PUBLISHING

ABOVE: *Aldus PageMaker was the first desktop publishing software, introduced in 1985 for the Apple Macintosh.*

OPPOSITE: *A selection of icons created by Susan Kare for the Apple Macintosh.*

For 1,500 years, paper and ink dominated written communication. The printing press ruled for another 500 years. In the mid-80s, Adobe, Apple and Aldus created a new paradigm – desktop publishing (DTP).

The home-publishing revolution began at Xerox PARC. Like many other PARC employees, John Warnock became frustrated at Xerox's refusal to market his innovation, so he left to form his own company. The product he had created was PostScript, a programming language to control the laser printer. The company he created was called Adobe Systems.

The same year, during the third quarter of Super Bowl XVIII, Apple aired its famous '1984' ad for the Macintosh. The Mac came bundled with two applications – MacWrite and MacPaint. Dismissed by many as a toy, the Apple Macintosh changed computing forever.

The following year, Aldus launched PageMaker for the Mac, the world's first DTP software. The Mac's monochrome screen was only 512 pixels wide by 342 high, but the seeds of the home-publishing revolution had been planted.

In 1987 came the release of the Macintosh II, with its larger colour screen, and QuarkXPress, which incorporated sophisticated typographic control and, crucially, image handling. This combination of hardware and software proved pivotal. It was not long before all publishing was desktop publishing.

At first, untrained amateurs polluted the world with poorly designed pamphlets, posters and logos. However, over time, enlightened graphic designers saw the potential of these new tools to create highly polished designs.

History repeated itself with the emergence of the Web. Slow connection speeds, limited fonts and a restricted colour palette put off most graphic designers from working on webpage design. Spoiled by a decade of sophisticated digital design tools, they were unwilling to compromise their craft. Another bunch of untrained amateurs were more than happy to fill the void.

In the same way that PageMaker had opened up graphic design to the masses in the mid-80s, WYSIWYG web-design software, such as Dreamweaver and GoLive, allowed anybody with a PC and modem to create webpages ten years later. The results were often horrific (anyone remember **GeoCities**?) but a generation had been empowered to self-publish. Now all publishing is self-publishing ■

'A programming tool for the rest of us'

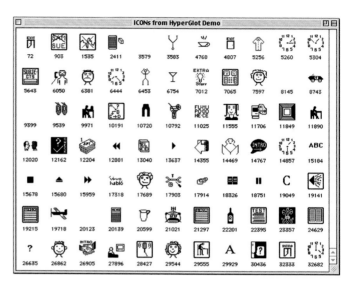

HYPERCARD

A screenshot from the HyperGlot language-teaching software, one of the many pieces of commercial software made on HyperCard.

The year 1987 saw the release of the Apple Macintosh II. Bundled with it was a piece of software called HyperCard. This was the world's first programming tool for non-programmers.

HyperCard was created by Bill Atkinson, who also created MacPaint. His aim was to 'bridge the gap between the priesthood of programmers and the Macintosh mouse clickers.' The software allowed users to create a stack of cards, populated with text, images, audio and video. What made HyperCard powerful was that cards could be linked to one another. For the more ambitious, HyperCard included a scripting language called HyperTalk, which incorporated commands like 'onMouseDown', 'go to' or 'play sound'. Aimed at novice programmers, it is a direct ancestor of languages like JavaScript, AppleScript and ActionScript that are still in use today.

All sorts of people and organizations used HyperCard to create applications, prototypes and interactive experiences that went far beyond Atkinson's expectations. The Voyager Company used it extensively to create interactive CD-ROMs. Renault used it to manage its inventory. Libraries used it to catalogue their collections. Schools and hospitals used it as a teaching aid. Perhaps the most famous example of a HyperCard project is Myst, the most popular desktop computer game of the 1990s.

Despite such widespread adoption, HyperCard was not a commercial success. Some people within Apple even thought it might be detrimentally affecting the sales of their software division, Claris. With the growth of the Web, HyperCard's popularity diminished and Apple sidelined the software. Macromedia stepped in to fill the void. Director, Flash

'Created to bridge the gap between the priesthood of programmers and the Macintosh mouse clickers.'

and Dreamweaver targeted non-programmers in the same way HyperCard had a decade earlier. This suite of software, which owes so much to HyperCard, allowed artists and designers to play their part in shaping the Web.

HyperCard was the first hypermedia program, directly influencing the Web, the browser and countless websites. Tim Berners-Lee credits HyperCard as a direct inspiration for Enquire, the **hypertext** program that evolved into the Web. Pei-Yuan Wei incorporated HyperCard functionality within his influential web browser, ViolaWWW. Ward Cunningham, the inventor of the **wiki**, says a HyperCard stack was his original inspiration.

Atkinson laments, 'I grew up in a box-centric culture at Apple. If I'd grown up in a network-centric culture, like Sun, HyperCard might have been the first web browser.' Despite this, HyperCard's legacy is apparent to all. The Web made the internet more accessible. The **browser** did the same for the Web. Neither of these leaps would have been made if Bill Atkinson had not made 'a programming tool for the rest of us.' ∎

ABOVE: A screenshot from The Manhole, a children's adventure game created using HyperTalk by Rand and Robyn Miller, who went on to create Myst.

'It's 20 years old. It supports only 256 colours. It's unsuitable for photographs. It has no sound capability. ... Yet the GIF is still hanging in there.'

Spirit of the Web

IDEA № 18
GRAPHICS INTERCHANGE FORMAT

Webpages, **social networks**, **blogs**, email, message boards, **banner ads**. Other than HTML, one thing is consistent across them all – the graphics interchange format (GIF).

It's 20 years old. It supports only 256 colours. It's unsuitable for photographs. It has no sound capability. It's inferior to the PNG (see below). Yet the GIF is still hanging in there. Why has it proved so tenacious? Because it can move.

CompuServe introduced the GIF format in the pre-Web days of 1987. It was released as a free and open specification for sharing colour images across their network.

A GIF supports 8 bits per pixel. This allows it to reference 256 distinct colours (2^8), chosen from a palette of millions. Each of these colours is stored in a table and given a value. When neighbouring pixels are the same colour, the run-length is specified followed by the colour value. This is called LZW data compression, after its creators Abraham Lempel, Jacob Ziv and Terry Welch. It means images can be downloaded reasonably quickly, even with slow modems.

LZW compression was described by Welch in the June 1984 issue of the Institute of Electrical and Electronics Engineers (IEEE) magazine. It soon became the most popular form of data compression. What the article did not mention was that Unisys held a patent on the algorithm.

GIFs really took off in 1993 with the release of Mosaic, the first graphical **browser**. Mosaic introduced the <img> tag, which supported two formats – GIF

and a black-and-white format called XBM. Mosaic became Netscape and, as it grew, the GIF grew with it.

In 1994, Unisys decided to enforce its patent, announcing that developers would have to pay a licence fee to use their algorithm. This caused outrage. It turned out that the patent covered the software that made GIFs, not the files themselves, but it was enough for a working group to come up with a new format, portable network graphics (PNG). The PNG was adopted by the World Wide Web Consortium (W3C) as a standard. The GIF looked doomed.

In 1996, Netscape 2.0 was released. It supported GIF animations – multiple frames shown in succession. The Web went crazy. Suddenly there were spinning logos, animated under-construction signs and dancing babies (see **Viral Content**) everywhere you looked. The PNG does not support animation.

The LZW patents expired in 2004. Since then, Myspace and Tumblr have attracted a new generation of GIF artists. Called 'the spirit of the Web' by artist and GIF model Olia Lialina (see **Net Art**), it is the limitations of the GIF that have made it so attractive. Within minutes, a GIF animation can be made and viewed, often without the need to click on a link. Sometimes the old ways are the best ways. ∎

ABOVE: Dancing Girl by legendary GIF artist Chuck Poynter.

OPPOSITE: GIF artwork created for German magazine Der Spiegel by eBoy.

Semi-colon dash closing parenthesis

THE EMOTICON

Since the beginning of written communication, symbols have been used to convey emotions. Early examples, used by telegraph operators, include '73' meaning 'best regards' and '88' meaning 'love and kisses'. On the Web the equivalent is an emoticon, a visual representation of a facial expression using punctuation marks, numbers and letters ;-)

In 1963 State Mutual Life hired cartoonist Harvey Ball to create a smiley face for the company's 'Friendship' campaign. He designed a circular yellow face with two black dots for eyes and a simple curve for a mouth. It took him ten minutes and he was paid $45. In 1970, brothers Bernard and Murray Spain added the line 'Have a Nice Day' and sold millions of dollars' worth of merchandise. Two years later, Franklin Loufrani gave the face a name and took the 'Smiley' to Paris, licensing it to French newspapers to highlight positive stories. Harvey Ball's design had gone global. When asked if he regretted not trademarking his design, Ball's response was philosophical: 'Hey, I can only eat one steak at a time.'

The first use of the smiley face on a screen was in 1982 at Carnegie Mellon University. Jokey remarks on the computer science department's online bulletin board were often misinterpreted and a 'flame war' would result. At best, the original intent of the thread was lost. At worst, people were offended. Research professor Scott Fahlman pragmatically suggested it would be a good idea to mark posts that were not to be taken seriously:

```
<19-Sep-82 11:44   Scott E  Fahlman   :)

From: Scott E Fahlman <Fahlman at Cmu-20c>
I propose that the following character sequence for joke
markers:
:-)
Read it sideways. Actually, it is probably more
economical to mark things that are NOT jokes - given
current trends. For this, use
:-(
```

The convention caught on and spread to other universities and research centres. The Smiley and other emoticons, like the wink ;-), grin :-D and tongue out :-P were very quickly in

(^_-)

common use on **bulletin boards** across **the internet**.

In the mid-'80s, Japanese internet users popularized a style of *emojis* that did not involve tilting your head, such as (*_*) and (^.^). Other examples include a wink (^_-) and confusion (@_@), while a stressful situation is represented by (-_-;), the semi-colon representing sweat!

When Web chat took off in the mid-'90s, emoticons evolved into images. Instant messaging services such as ICQ and AOL Instant Messenger started offering a wide range of icons that could be inserted into text at the click of a mouse. In 1997, Franklin Loufrani's son, Nicolas created a dictionary of animated GIF icons, based on the Smiley, to replace text-based emoticons. There are now over 2,000 icons in this dictionary and, to the annoyance of many, modern platforms often auto-replace text-based emoticons with these animated images.

Of the phenomenon he created, Scott Fahlman says wearily, 'I had no idea that I was starting something that would soon pollute all the world's communication channels.' I like to think that, in his head at least, this statement ends with a smiley face. ∎

50,000 trillion trillion addresses per person. That should be enough.

IDEA № 20

THE DOMAIN NAME SYSTEM

The Domain Name System (DNS) is a system for identifying a device connected to the internet. It translates numerical IP addresses into easily memorized domain names.

In the early days, there were only a few hosts (computers) connected to the internet. Each had a numerical address, listed in a central text file maintained by Stanford Research Institute. Everyone on the network had to copy the host.txt file daily to get the latest version. As more networks joined **the internet**, this became impractical.

In 1983, Paul Mockapetris was set the task of designing a scaleable way of assigning and recording internet addresses. He came up with the Domain Name System we still use today.

His solution distributes the responsibility of assigning domain names. Authoritative name servers have responsibility for top-level domains, like .com or .net. These authoritative name servers then assign registrars to administer second-level domains, like google.com. Once a second-level domain name is assigned, its local network administrator can add subdomains, for example mail.google.com.

The first generic, top-level domains were implemented on 1 January 1985. They were .com, .net, .org, .edu, .gov and .mil. The first domain name was registered the same day – nordu.net, a Nordic research network. The first . com address was symbolics.com, registered by Symbolics Computers on 15 March 1985. In the first two years, fewer than 100 companies registered their domains; those with the foresight to do so included IBM and Intel. Apple, Adobe. Many others had joined the race by 1987, but it was the birth of the Web that created a domain name gold rush. The most expensive domain names ever purchased are insure.com (bought for $16 million in 2009) and sex.com (bought for $14 million in 2010).

The first widely deployed internet protocol was IPv4. This was designed to handle up to 4 billion IP addresses, an inconceivably large number in 1981. However, the Web had not been invented then. By the early '90s it was obvious that IP addresses would eventually run out.

IPv6 was approved in 1995 and has been available since 2004. It accommodates 340 undecillion addresses, which is 50,000 trillion trillion per person on the planet. That is quite a lot. Even with the ever-increasing

'Without DNS, there is no dot-com and without dot-com, there is no dot-com revolution.'

As more and more devices are connected to the internet, the demand for IP addresses increases.

number of new devices being connected to the internet, this should be enough for some time to come. However, more addresses means longer IP numbers, which means changing all **TCP/IP** routing software – a major alteration to the underlying architecture of the Web. As a result, IPv6 currently accounts for only 1 per cent of IP addresses. This will have to change.

DNS servers receive billions of simultaneous requests. Millions of domain names and IP addresses are changed every day. DNS handles all of these with ease, yet its importance is more fundamental than that. Without DNS, there would have been no dot-com, and without dot-com, there would have been no dot-com revolution. ∎

IDEA № 21

THE PROJECT

In March 1989, while working at CERN, the British scientist Tim Berners-Lee recognized that although CERN was nominally organized in a hierarchical structure, it was in fact an interconnected web. It needed an information-sharing system to match. He proposed using hyperlinks to connect and share documents over the **internet**. He called this idea The Project.

Most of the technology for the Project already existed. People had been sharing information over the internet for a decade or so. **Hypertext** and **markup language** had been around since the 60s. **The Domain Name System** was up and running. Berners-Lee has since said, 'I just had to take the hypertext idea and connect it to the **Transmission Control Protocol** and domain name system ideas and ta-da! The World Wide Web.' On 6 August 1991, with the help of Robert Cailliau, Berners-Lee published the first website. Visitors to the site learnt how to create a webpage, use a **browser** and set up a web server. Initially, the Web was far from worldwide. It was only accessible by a handful of people at CERN who had a NeXT computer. This was soon to change. By the end of 1992 the Web was global.

Its popularity was due to its simplicity. It was, and still is, easy to link to another page. The use of one-way links drew criticism from some. Ted Nelson raged, 'Ever-breaking links and links going outward were precisely what we were trying to prevent' (see **Xanadu**),

but the genie was out of the bottle. The Web received a further boost in 1993 with the release of Mosaic (see **Web Browser**), which extended the reach of the Web beyond computer scientists and academics. The same year, the University of Minnesota announced that it would start charging for Gopher, a widely adopted internet search-and-retrieval tool. Users switched to the Web en masse.

The invention of the World Wide Web was celebrated at the Opening Ceremony of the London 2012 Olympic Games.

'I just had to take the hypertext idea and connect it to the Transmission Control Protocol and domain name system ideas and ta-da! The World Wide Web.'

If the internet is the digital equivalent of the printing press, the Web is moveable type. Just as moveable type allowed the accumulated knowledge of the human race to reach every person who could read, the Web extends this knowledge to everyone with access to a computer. And just as the Gutenberg Bible signified the start of the Industrial Age, the Web signals the birth of the Information Age. ■

A live portrait of Tim Berners-Lee (an early warning system) *by Thomson and Craighead, 2012, commissioned by the National Media Museum in Bradford, UK.*

'A map to the buried treasures of the Information Age'

IDEA № 22

WEB BROWSER

At the end of 1992 there were 50 websites in the world. Five years later there were a million. The reason for this rapid growth was the web browser.

The Mosaic browser, the world's first cross-platform point-and-click browser.

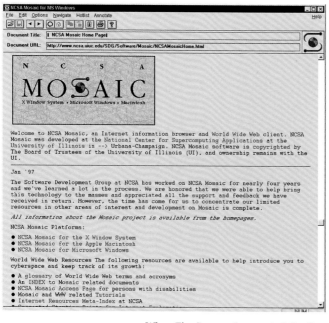

When Tim Berners-Lee created the first webpage, he also created the first web browser (see **The Project**). He called it WorldWideWeb, later renaming it the Nexus browser. The crucial point about his browser was that it was a browser-editor. Not only did it allow visitors from the local server to view a page, but

also it allowed them to edit it. This was a key part of Berners-Lee's vision. He envisaged the Web as a multi-author environment.

The Nexus browser ran only on the NeXTstep operating system. A more widely accessible version was needed fast. As a short-term measure, Berners-Lee asked Nicola Pellow, a student intern at CERN, to write a read-only browser. It was called Line Mode. Browsers have been passive ever since.

In 1992, inspired by Bill Atkinson's **HyperCard**, Pei-Yuan Wei released ViolaWWW. It was the first graphical browser. Viola's functionality was ahead of the game, but it only worked on Unix. In 1993, Marc Andreessen and Eric Bina created the Mosaic browser, the world's first cross-platform point-and-click browser. Described by the *New York Times* as 'a map to the buried treasures of the Information Age ... so obviously useful that it can create a new industry from scratch', Mosaic changed everything. The Web was no longer the exclusive domain of academics. Developed at the University of Illinois' National Center for Supercomputing Applications (NCSA), it quickly became the Web's most popular browser.

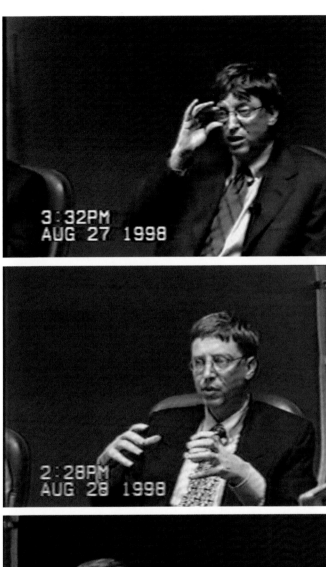

Bill Gates testifying in the 1998 United States versus Microsoft Corporation anti-trust case, where Microsoft was accused of engaging in monopolistic practices.

In 1994, Marc Andreessen left NCSA and formed Netscape Communications with Jim Clark, one of the founders of Silicon Graphics. They launched Netscape Navigator the same year with the campaign, 'The Web is for everyone'. The company went public in November 1995, the shares more than doubling in value on the first day of trading. It was a sign of things to come.

Microsoft reacted decisively. It licensed the Mosaic code and released Internet Explorer, but it was a long way behind – Netscape had 86 per cent of the market. Microsoft decided to play tough. It shipped Internet Explorer as part of Windows 95. Netscape could not compete. With nothing to lose, in 1998 it released the code under an open-source licence. Mozilla 1.0 was released in 2002 but it failed to catch on. In 2004, a slimmer version was released – Mozilla Firefox – which quickly captured a quarter of the browser market.

Twenty years on, Apple's Safari and Google Chrome have joined the browser wars. What is remarkable is how similar today's browsers are to Mosaic, the Web's first killer app. ∎

'Cookies save users having to enter the same information repeatedly. '

Don't look now, but you are being followed

IDEA № 23
THE COOKIE

Every webpage you visit, every file you download, every link you click is scrutinized and recorded. The innocuous technology that makes this possible is a simple text file called a cookie.

A cookie is a small set of data sent from a web server and stored on a user's computer. It records log-in details, preferences and pages visited. When a user revisits a site, the data stored in the cookie is retrieved. The website then uses this information to tailor the experience, avoiding the need for users to enter the same information repeatedly.

Lou Montulli, who wrote a large chunk of the code for Netscape Navigator, invented the cookie. One of his many challenges was how to support e-commerce, particularly partially completed transactions. For security reasons, he did not want the information stored on the server. He needed to find a way to store the information on the user's computer instead. His solution was the cookie.

Web cookies get their name from 'magic cookies', tokens exchanged by computer programs to confirm a data transaction. They can be compared to a cloakroom ticket. The ticket has no intrinsic meaning but it can be exchanged for the correct coat when returned to the cloakroom. Likewise, cookies usually contain only a website address and an arbitrary number for identification.

When a single website issues a cookie, there are no privacy concerns.

It gets more complicated when a third party issues a cookie. Using the cloakroom analogy, if a third party issues cloakroom tickets, suddenly they have a record of everywhere you have stored your coat. Advertisers use this information to create a profile of an individual's browsing habits so they can target ads accordingly. As far back as 1997, the Internet Engineering Task Force recommended that third-party cookies be banned, a recommendation that was ignored by Netscape and Explorer – the Web had already become dependent on advertising.

Cookies continue to cause debate. First-party cookies are undoubtedly useful and pose very little threat to privacy. Third-party cookies help to keep the Web free. In the end, the individual needs to make the decision whether to accept them or not. What everyone agrees on, though, is that users need to know the facts to be able to do this. ∎

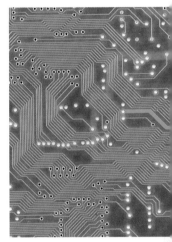

For security reasons, cookies are stored on the user's computer rather than on the Web server.

An image showing the effects of
compression damage to a jpeg file
(right-hand side).

A billion photographs uploaded every day can't be wrong

IDEA № 24
THE JPEG

The Joint Photographic Experts Group established the JPEG compression format in 1991. It is now the most common format for storing and sharing photographic images on the Web.

The JPEG uses 'lossy' compression. This compression technique reduces file size by discarding (losing) data. Often, a substantial amount of data can be discarded before the resulting degradation is noticeable by the user. Lossy compression is most commonly used to compress images, video and audio data. 'Lossless' compression is used for text and data files.

There are two approaches to lossy compression. Sometimes file size can be reduced without affecting the perception of image quality. At other times, a perceptible loss of image quality is considered a valid trade-off for a reduced file size. The degree of compression can be adjusted, allowing a selectable trade-off between image quality and storage size.

Repeated compression of lossy compression formats, such as the JPEG, results in generative loss (a progressive loss of quality). This is in contrast with lossless data compression, such as **GIF**, where no data is lost. The advantage of lossy over lossless compression, though, is that smaller file sizes can be generated, while still meeting the requirements of the file.

The JPEG compression algorithm works in a number of stages. Firstly, the colour range is halved, moving from 512 variations of colours to 256. This is imperceptible to the human eye. The image is then divided into 8 x 8-pixel blocks. For each block, the maximum compression is 64:1. The importance of each block to the overall image is then assessed. The human eye is more sensitive to low-frequency colours, such as reds and yellows, than to high-frequency colours, such as blues and greens. Low-frequency colours are therefore compressed less than high-frequency colours. The retina is also very good at identifying areas of high contrast. When a block is made up of pixels that are relatively bright compared to nearby pixels they are also deemed important and compressed less. The resulting data for all 8 x 8 blocks is further compressed with a lossless algorithm; 8 red pixels in a row become 8R rather than RRRRRRRR.

JPEG compression works best on images of various tones, such as photographs. It is not suitable for illustrations. Distinct contrasts between adjacent pixels result in noticeable artefacts, or 'noise'. The GIF format is a more suitable compression format in this instance.

Over a billion photographs are uploaded to the Web every day. The majority are JPEGs. Without this compression technique, file sizes would be at least 15 times larger. Fifteen times the data means 15 times the wait. And nobody wants that. ∎

> 'Operating outside normal business constraints and with huge financial rewards, the porn industry was able to innovate.'

An example of early ASCII pornn.

Innovation's dirty secret

IDEA № 25
PORNOGRAPHY

Every time you buy something online, watch a video on YouTube, upload a piece of user-generated content or chat with someone via Skype, you should say a quiet thank you to the porn industry.

In the early days of **the internet**, before the birth of the Web, conversations and file sharing took place on **bulletin board systems** (BBSs). It was not long before images scanned from magazines were uploaded and shared with scant regard for copyright. Even in the early 90s, before there were graphics on the Web, enterprising individuals were creating pornographic pictures using ASCII symbols. In the mid-'90s, when browsers started to support images, despite the horrendously slow download speeds, the demand for porn exploded.

One of the earliest adult sites was created by ex-stripper Danni Ashe, the only woman in the world to have appeared on the cover of both the *Wall Street Journal* and *Juggs*. After reading Nicholas Negroponte's *Being Digital* in 1995, Ashe decided to create her own website. Two weeks later she had created danni.com, otherwise known as Danni's Hard Drive. The site launched in July 1995, with subscribers paying $9.95 a month to access soft-core pornographic pictures. The site crashed immediately due to the huge number of visitors. While investors poured billions into loss-making dot-com businesses, Danni's Hard Drive was quietly making millions of dollars. Operating outside normal business constraints and with huge financial rewards, sites like danni.com were able to innovate. The porn industry created the first online payment systems and continually pushed technology beyond its recognized boundaries.

The only thing on the Web more popular than pornographic images was moving pornographic images. As modem speeds improved, the adult industry was quick to react. Ten years before YouTube, adult sites were streaming videos. The natural next step was webcams. The same technology that brought live nude girls to your screen laid the foundation for today's video-conferencing software. Just as pornographic content helped popularize cable TV, impatient visitors to adult sites were soon demanding faster connection speeds. Modem makers struggled to keep up.

Even today, online businesses look to porn for innovation. As well as pioneering teledildonics (yep, you guessed it), the adult industry is one of the leading developers of anti-piracy software. If you want to know what is round the corner, watch the porn industry. Just make sure you activate 'private browsing' first. ∎

Danni Ashe, founder of Danni's Hard Drive.

Links are the currency of the Web

IDEA № 26
SEARCH

In the early days of the Web, Tim Berners-Lee maintained a list of websites on the CERN web server. This was fine at the beginning of 1992, when there were 26. By the end of 1994 there were more than 10,000.

Google founders, Sergey Brin and Larry Page.

The first search engine was developed before the Web. 'Archie' (short for 'archive') searched FTP sites on the internet. Other search engines followed, but it was not until 1995 that an engine emerged that crawled, indexed and ranked websites. By 1997, AltaVista was the most popular page on the Web and was handling more than 20 million queries a day.

A number of other search engines followed the AltaVista model. Excite, Infoseek, Lycos and Magellan all returned results based on keywords. However, by 1998 there were millions of websites, and search results deteriorated as a result. To maintain quality, Yahoo! bucked the trend and used people to create their search directory.

A couple of Stanford students, Sergey Brin and Larry Page, saw an opportunity. Yahoo!'s model was unsustainable, and relying on keywords was not accurate enough, but how else could results be measured? Brin and Page took their inspiration from the academic world they lived in. The value of an academic paper is judged by peer approval, or how many times the paper is referenced. On paper, those references appear as footnotes. On the Web, they appear as links. The two students came up with the PageRank algorithm, ranking results based on the number of incoming links rather than the number of keywords. A beta (trial) site, run from a friend's garage, instantly began returning better results than commercial search engines. The future of the Web had arrived. It was called Google.

The quest for a smarter search engine is ongoing, with Google at the helm. First there was semantic search, based on previous behaviour. Then there was social search, based on what your friends are searching for. Now, with Google Glass, there is augmented search, where Google can see and hear, as well as read.

Baidu and Yandex hold their own in China and Russia, but Google is still the search engine of choice for nine out of ten people around the world. Whatever the future holds for search, you can be sure that Google and its PageRank algorithm will play a role. ■

'In 1998, the future of the Web had arrived. It was called Google.'

The thousands of metres of pipe that line the inside of Google data centres are painted in the Google colours not only because it's fun, but also to designate which is which.

Hollywood actress Hedy Lamarr, inventor of frequency-hopping spread spectrum radio, the technology that underpins WiFi.

Spreading the signal

WIFI

In 1933, the most popular film was *King Kong*, but the most talked about was *Ecstasy*, a Czechoslovakian film featuring the first onscreen orgasm. Its leading lady went on to invent the technology that underpins WiFi.

Following her performance in *Ecstasy*, Hedy Kiestler married the arms dealer, Friedrich Mandl, the richest man in Austria. Mandl took his beautiful wife to business meetings to impress his clients – senior officials of the German and Italian fascist governments. A recurring subject of conversation was how to stop the enemy from jamming the signal of radio-guided torpedoes. Whoever managed such a feat would control the seas. Jewish-born Hedy, with a secret love of science, quietly set her mind to coming up with the solution.

In 1937, tired of her domineering husband, Hedy fled to Hollywood. She changed her name to Hedy Lamarr and forged a hugely successful acting career. Alongside Victor Mature, she was the star of the box-office smash, *Samson and Delilah*. During this period she visited the eccentric composer George Antheil for advice about improving her figure. Somehow, torpedoes came up. Hedy told him about her idea for a radio signal that hopped frequencies. Antheil suggested that a hole-punched ribbon, similar to the paper roll in a player piano, could advise the transmitter and receiver of the changing frequencies. A year later, in 1941, they registered a patent for a 'secret communication system' that constantly switched frequency.

Thirty years later, in 1971, at the University of Hawaii, a computer network was created based on this technology. Called ALOHAnet, it used radio signals to connect computers across the Hawaiian Islands. A dedicated radio frequency would mean only one message could be sent at once. By spreading the signal across the spectrum, several computers could communicate simultaneously without interfering with one another. It was the world's first wireless network.

The term WiFi was coined by Interbrand in 1999, and we have not looked back since. Liberated from our desks, we use WiFi to surf the Web, send email, find our location and make phone calls. Wireless networking has taken the Web **mobile**.

The next time you make a call or use a WiFi network, say a quiet thank you to a beautiful actress with a head for numbers. ∎

'Immaterials: Light painting WiFi' by Timo Arnall, Jørn Knutsen and Einar Sneve Martinussen at the Oslo School of Architecture & Design explores the invisible terrain of WiFi networks by light-painting signal strength in long-exposure photographs.

Many heads are better than one

IDEA № 28
OPEN SOURCE

The concept of giving away information existed long before computers. From recipes to storytelling, knowledge-sharing and building on other people's ideas are a fundamental part of human culture.

Until the mid-'60s, openness and cooperation typified the software industry. Software was produced collectively, adhering to principles established in the field of academia. This collaborative process led to the birth of both the internet and the Web.

By the '70s the software industry had developed beyond hardware manufacturers. Specialist companies were challenging the bundled hardware-and-software model. By the early '80s, led by Microsoft, charging a licence fee for software became the norm. AT&T followed suit. In 1984, it started charging a licence fee for its widely used UNIX operating system, which was originally distributed for free.

Richard Stallman, a programmer at MIT, was incensed. He responded by founding the Free Software Foundation and initiating the GNU Project, a recursive acronym for 'GNUs Not UNIX!' His aim was to create a free alternative to UNIX. For Stallman, it was a question of fundamental rights. In his words, 'Free software is a matter of liberty, not price. To understand the concept, you should think of free speech, not free beer.' He had sown the seeds of a software revolution.

After a positive start, development of GNU slowed down. The crucial master program that would control the OS, the kernel, was proving elusive. Step forward a 21-year-old student at the University of Helsinki. In 1991, Linus Torvalds wrote some software to enable his PC to access the university's UNIX servers. He called it Freax and made the code available for other programmers to use and improve. Renamed 'Linux' in honour of its creator, GNU now had its missing kernel.

In 1997, Eric Raymond published an essay called 'The Cathedral and the Bazaar', which told the story of Linux and extolled the virtues of open source. The heart of the essay can be summed up by what Raymond calls Linus's Law: 'Given enough eyeballs, all bugs are shallow.' This essay was read with interest by Netscape's management team. After losing the browser war to Microsoft Explorer, Netscape released its code as open source. Today's Firefox **browser**, used by one in five people, is based on open-source Netscape code.

Software like Linux, Firefox, PHP and Apache proves that, often, the best choice is open source, but it is not a one-way street. Some of the most successful companies in the world pursue a licensing model, Microsoft, Apple and Adobe among them. What the open-source movement does is offer a viable alternative. ■

Richard Stallman, Open Source pioneer and founder of the GNU Project.

In 1993, AOL offered access to USENET and flooded it with thousands of new users. In previous years the September influx of students learned the ropes by October and 11 months of relative stability followed. This was no longer the case, the newbies just kept coming. Now known as the 'Eternal September', it was a pivotal point in the mass adoption of the Net. Pictured here, the German chapter of the 'No More AOL CDs' campaign.

Remember, remember, before the Eternal September

NETIQUETTE

In a world without facial expressions and body language, it is easy to offend people without meaning to, and to take offence when it is not intended. To avoid this, a code of behaviour has been established that guides the way that we communicate online.

How we politely use new technology is not a new conundrum. When the telephone was invented, people were often silent when they picked up the receiver, waiting for the caller to introduce themselves before they spoke. Eventually, we learnt to say 'hello'.

Like the telephone, the Web has its own social conventions. People quickly realized that, online, humour and sarcasm had to be used with care. Insulting exchanges, known as flame wars, were common on the early Net, and sideways smiley faces started appearing to make sure jokes were not misinterpreted (see **The Emoticon**). Many other inventive uses of typography to portray facial expressions followed. Emoticons are now an essential part of our online vocabulary.

The first generation of Net users also established other conventions to keep things civil. Some are obvious. Read the FAQs before asking a question. Writing in caps is TANTAMOUNT TO SHOUTING. Criticizing people's grammar is irritating. Hijacking a discussion thread is plain rude. Others are less obvious. Unnecessarily long responses waste people's time. Compulsory fields on forms should be kept to a minimum. Telling people to 'click here' is patronizing.

As the Web evolves, so do the social conventions that govern it. With online maps at our fingertips, it is no longer acceptable to ask for directions, and RTFM (read the f***ing manual) has been replaced with LMGTFY (let me Google that for you).

But it's social networks that offer the real opportunities for digital faux pas. When clothing company Kenneth Cole joked on Twitter 'Millions are in uproar in #CAIRO. Rumor has it they heard our new spring collection is available online', it was not well received. Equally, the furniture store Habitat caused outrage when it hijacked a hashtag associated with the Iranian elections. Tweets promoting soft furnishings appearing among messages of police brutality caused widespread offence.

This new way of interacting can be daunting, but ultimately the rules are very simple. Adhere to the same standards of behaviour online that you follow in real life and you will not go far wrong ;-) ∎

'A last stand against the commercialization of the Web.'

APACHE WEB SERVER

Apache is the most popular web server software in the world, delivering around two-thirds of all websites. Incredibly, thanks to a 21-year-old university drop-out from California, it is free, hacked together by a loose coalition of volunteer programmers.

Brian Behlendorf, open-source hero and creator of the Apache web server.

In 1993, Marc Andreessen and Eric Bina created the world's first graphical browser, Mosaic. This changed everything. Suddenly, the Web was no longer the exclusive domain of academics and computer geeks (see **Web Browser**).

Developed at the University of Illinois' National Center for Supercomputing Applications, alongside the Mosaic browser, was the NCSA web server. Programmed by undergraduate Rob McCool, it quickly became the server of choice for those launching the first wave of commercial websites. One of these young webmasters, setting up *Wired* magazine's first website, Hotwired, was 21-year-old university drop-out Brian Behlendorf.

The NCSA web server was not perfect – its password authentication module did not quite meet *Wired's* requirements. So, like many webmasters at the time, Behlendorf rolled up his sleeves and wrote a patch that fixed the problem. Previously, he would have sent the patch to McCool for inclusion in the next release of the program, but McCool and the original Mosaic team at NCSA had departed en masse to Silicon Valley, many of them lured by Marc Andreessen to Netscape.

Behlendorf could see the Web going the same way as the desktop, monopolized by a single company, and was determined to do what he could to ensure that a robust, feature-rich web server remained publicly available. He knew other webmasters were writing their own NCSA fixes, so he contacted a few, suggesting that they join forces to collect all the updates in one place and overhaul the NCSA code themselves.

Seven programmers answered Behlendorf's call, and by April 1995 they had completely rewritten the program. Because they represented a

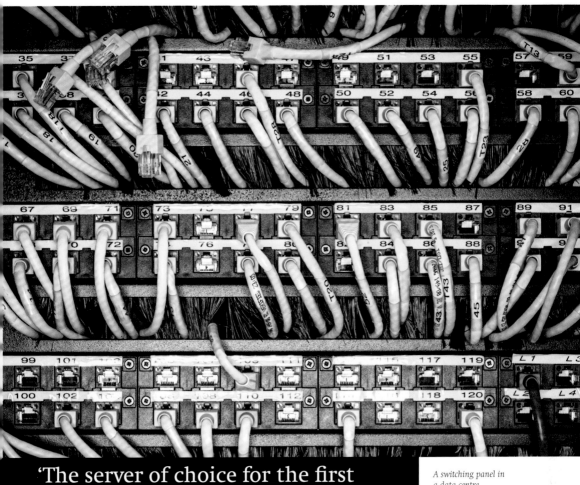

'The server of choice for the first wave of commercial websites.'

A switching panel in a data centre.

last stand against the commercialization of the web, the team became the Apache Group. It was also a convenient pun, their rewritten code being 'a patchy server'. Less than a year later, in December 1995, Apache surpassed the NCSA server as the most popular on the internet – a position it retains today.

Now run as a not-for-profit corporation, the Apache Software Foundation still adheres to its original principles, the ideals of the gift economy practised by Behlendorf and his fellow open-source pioneers.

As for Behlendorf himself, he is now CTO at the World Economic Forum, showing business and political leaders how they can improve the world through the participatory, gifting culture of the open-source movement that gave birth to the Apache web server. ∎

The foundation of the self-publishing revolution

CONTENT MANAGEMENT SYSTEMS

A content management system (CMS) allows the centralized creation, editing and publishing of web pages. The introduction of CMS allowed non-technical people, with little or no knowledge of HTML, to update and maintain websites.

In a typical CMS, page content and metadata are stored in a database. This is known as the data layer. A presentation layer, usually consisting of a series of templates, is used to display the data. The logic that manipulates the data and determines how it is displayed is known as the business layer. The presentation and business layer are usually fixed. The CMS allows users to add content in the data layer.

Administration is typically done through a browser-based interface. With varied levels of access, different users can manage different pages and different bits of functionality. A web developer will usually set up and add pages, which are then maintained by non-technical editors. A CMS can also incorporate workflow management tools. For example, an editor may create a page and a proofreader then check it before it is published by the website administrator.

Content management systems can also act as platforms for collaboration, with pages created by multiple authors. Version control means editors can revert to previous iterations when required.

Content management systems emerged in the mid-90s. One of the early platforms was StoryServer, built by a company called Vignette; it was a combination of Vignette's own product, StoryBuilder, and a rival CMS called PRISM. StoryServer and other CMS's offered an alternative to conventional page-by-page web development. They signalled a maturing of the Web, allowing non-technical people to manage websites.

However, this freedom came at a cost. Enterprise CMSs were extremely expensive. Smaller businesses, design agencies and independent software companies started creating their own open-source CMSs based on the LAMP (Linux, Apache, MySQL, PHP) framework. One of these companies was UserLand, the company that gave us the **Blog**. It distributed its Frontier software as shareware, allowing users to 'taste the power of large-scale database publishing with free software'.

Open-source CMSs, such as Joomla and Drupal, now dominate the market. Blogging platforms, such as WordPress, have adopted much of their functionality and today power many websites.

Content management systems laid the foundations of the self-publishing

Content management systems are used to manage the web-publishing process as well as to upload and edit content.

revolution. They allowed anyone with a PC and an internet connection to publish a website. Without them, the Web would be the sole domain of people who know how to code – a far cry from the universal space envisaged by Tim Berners-Lee. ∎

DIGITAL
Archaeology

Search   🔍

THE IDEA OF THE INTERNET WAS BORN IN BELGIUM

April 11th, 2013 ...

Blog – Edit...

In 1934, six decades before the birth of the web, a Belgian bibliophile described his **vision for** *té lé photographie*, an electronic telescope which could transmit any document in the **world to a** television screen.

Paul Otlet loved libraries. In 1895 he met a kindred spirit, fellow Belgian and future Nobel Prize winner, Henri La Fontaine. Together they conceived The Mundaneum, a comprehensive collection of the world's published knowledge, equal in ambition to the great Library of Alexandria.

The telegraph room at The Mundaneum

By 1910 they had collected thousands of books, newspapers, photographs, journals, posters and postcards. Otlet called the collection the *ré seau*, a network of documents connected by *links*. More than blind signposts, these links described the relationships between documents, an implementation of what we now call the semantic web. As the Mundaneum grew, this degree of annotation became unmanageable. Otlet put his mind to new technologies that would overcome the limitations of paper-based records. In his 1934 book, *Monde*, he describes *"...a machinery unaffected by distance which would combine at the same time radio, X-rays, cinema and microscopic photography... From afar anyone would be able to read any passage, that would be projected onto his individual screen, thus in his armchair, anyone would be able to contemplate the whole of creation or particular parts of it."*

Otlet even predicted social networks and the mobile web with remarkable accuracy, expecting users to *"participate, applaud, give ovations and sing in the chorus"* and *"carry, in his or her pocket, a tiny little handset that will be tuned with the turn of a screw to the wavelength adopted by each emitting centre."*

Otlet died in 1944 with his life's work in ruins, his collection destroyed to make way for an exhibition of Third Reich art. Following the war, he was almost forgotten as American pioneers such as Vannevar ... ...elson came to the foreground. It wasn't until W. Boyd Rayward ... the prescience of his work became apparent.

... Otlet and Henri La Fontaine as their spiritual forefathers. Vinton Cerf, ... r of the Internet, says it as it is, *"The idea of the Internet was born in*

For those who don't like numbers, heat maps illustrate at a glance where people click.

'Social media has been called "the largest and most honest unselfconscious focus group in the world."'

RECENT POPULAR

Viewpoint: The Argument

Hey you, Get Off Of My Cloud

The secret history of WiFi

When CERN came to visit

Error 404: Digital Shoreditch 2013

TAGS

Web Agencies Web

Archiving Web History

Websites

ARCHIVES

September 2013
August 2013
July 2013
May 2013
April 2013
February 2013
December 2012
November 2012
October 2012
September 2012
August 2012
June 2011
November 2010

LASTEST TWEETS

"The best idea I've heard for that silly Internet thing" David Letterman interviewing JenniCam's Jennifer Rigley http://t.co/UCDCd9CTAX
09:21:15 AM September 10, 2013 from web

"Ready or not, computers are coming... that's good news, maybe the best since psychedelics" Stewart Brand 1972 http://t.co/KM5g4n3Hob
12:15:24 PM September 04, 2013 from web

...es Martinet, the ..., at John Lewis on ...rday http://t.co
...03, 2013 from web

... on 1,337 followers

LINKS WE LOVE

> *'In God we trust.*
> *All others must bring data.'*
>
> W. Edwards Deming, statistician

IDEA № 32

WEB ANALYTICS

The inventor of the department store, John Wanamaker, was the first person to buy advertising space in newspapers. He famously said, 'Half the money I spend on advertising is wasted, the trouble is, I don't know which half.'

That was before the Web was invented, the most measurable medium the world has ever known. The collection and reporting of website visitor data is called web analytics. The earliest online measurement tools, common across GeoCities in the mid-90s, were milometer-style hit counters. These days, web analytics is an industry in its own right.

At a basic level, you can measure the number of people who visit your site, and what the most popular pages are. Dig a little deeper and you can discover entrance and exit pages, the number of repeat visitors and the number of pages viewed per visit. 'Bounce rate' is a favoured measure. It reveals how many people came to your site and disappeared without getting beyond the homepage. If it is high, you are either attracting the wrong visitors or not providing the right content. Either way, your website is not working!

For those who do not like numbers, heat maps illustrate at a glance where people are clicking. Visualizations show that users often read webpages in an F-shaped pattern: they scan the top of the page, then make a horizontal sweep across the middle before skimming down the left-hand margin. Collecting this information allows you to make informed decisions about where to place the most important content on a page.

In addition to the huge amount of data that can be collected about visitor behaviour on your website, further analysis can also identify what happens off your website. Links from other sites, search engines, emails, banner ads and social networks can all be tracked.

Links from other sites tell you who your friends are and where else your audience hangs out. By looking at search logs you can see the keywords that led people to your site. This helps guide the type of content you provide and the language you should use. Stats from email and banner campaigns reveal how successful your marketing efforts are. Social media has been called 'the largest and most honest unselfconscious focus group in the world' – just be careful what you look for.

We have more data than ever before. The trick is not to measure everything you can, but to collect the data that will lead to meaningful insights. As with a Formula 1 car, lots of small tweaks can make a huge difference to the performance of the overall machine. ∎

'You haven't lived until you've died in MUD'

IDEA № 33

MASSIVELY MULTI-PLAYER ONLINE GAMING

When student friends Roy Trubshaw and Richard Bartle created Multi-User Dungeon at Essex University in the late '70s, they created not only a multi-player game, but also a parallel universe, a virtual world with all the emotions and complexities of planet Earth but without the physical limitations. And with added wizards and dragons to keep it interesting.

Blizzard Entertainment's World of Warcraft is the world's most subscribed MMORPG.

Roy Trubshaw was a keen player of adventure games, the genre of computer games named after Colossal Cave Adventure, created by Will Crowther in 1975. The game describes the area you are standing in, and lists nearby objects, characters and exits. The player has to figure out what to do next – 'take armour', 'attack wizard', 'go North', etc. Trubshaw loved the games' intellectual challenge but missed the player versus player element of the offline equivalent, Dungeons & Dragons. His response was to create Multi-User Dungeon. Also known as Essex MUD (and later, MUD1), it was an adventure game with real-time, multiplayer interaction.

When Trubshaw left Essex University in 1980, his friend Richard Bartle took over development of the game, greatly expanding and improving it. In 1983, Essex University allowed remote access to its network and Essex MUD soon had a global player base. Just as Colossal Cave Adventure had done before it, MUD1, spawned a new genre of computer game – also called the Multi-User Dungeon (MUD). Graphical versions like Island of Kesmai on CompuServe and Habitat on AOL (then known as Q-Link) soon followed.

With the faster connection speeds of the 90s, MUD became MMORPG, or 'massively multiplayer online role-playing game'. Rather then tens or perhaps hundreds of concurrent players, thousands of players could inhabit the virtual worlds of Neverwinter Nights or Ultima Online at any one time. The genre was even more popular in Asia. The South Korean game Nexus: The Kingdom of the Winds, released in 1996, had more than a million subscribers. EverQuest, launched in 1999, brought MMORPGs

into the Western mainstream, while Blizzard Entertainment's World of Warcraft (WoW), launched in 2004, is the most played game in the world, with over 10 million subscribers.

These massive virtual worlds provide unexpected insights. In WoW, when a player attacks Hakkar the Soulflayer, they catch an energy-sapping disease known as Corrupted Blood. The disease is caught simply by being near an infected player, and it kills low-level players in seconds. When it was first introduced, entire servers were infected within hours and huge numbers of players were wiped out. Eventually, the game's creators had to step in to contain the disease. The spread of the virus and players' reactions provided a model of how mass populations might react when faced with a real-world epidemic. MMORPGs are now watched with interest by the scientific community.

Online and offline behaviour do not always coincide, though. In the virtual space, gender, age, ethnicity and physical ability recede. Players are judged on their behaviour rather than their appearance. Many exhibit very different personalities online compared to AFK (away from keyboard). The story of a LegendMUD player called Karyn is revealing. After a two-month absence from the game, a letter from her parents claimed she had died in a car crash. Many of her online friends were upset and created a virtual garden of remembrance. They were no longer playing a game. Their grief was real. Later it became apparent that Karyn was probably a man and still alive, but many of the players still felt the same sense of loss.

As we spend more time online, the line between the real and the virtual will fade. Online communities may fill the void left by the demise of the local community. We will perhaps be less inhibited and more likely to find like-minded souls. Whatever the subtle shifts in our identity may be, we would do well to remember the old bulletin-board expression, 'You haven't lived until you've died in MUD'. ■

You've been framed

IDEA Nº 34
WEBCAM

The first use of a webcam was not for human communication but simply to see if the coffee had all gone.

Justin Kan, whose attempt to broadcast his entire life at Justin.tv popularized the term 'lifecasting'.

It all started back in 1991 at Cambridge University's Computer Laboratory. Hard-working students faced a perilous situation on a daily basis. Could they make it to the coffee pot before all the coffee was gone?

Quentin Stafford-Fraser worked in the Trojan Room. The coffee pot lived in the hallway just outside. He set up a camera facing the pot and ran wires under the floor to his computer. His friend Paul Jardetzky wrote a program that captured images of the pot every 30 seconds. No longer would Quentin and Paul and their fellow students make the journey to the coffee pot in vain. Two years later, in November 1993, students Daniel Gordon and Martyn Johnson adapted the program so the coffee pot could be seen via a standard Web browser. The Trojan Room coffee pot became an international sensation overnight.

The first commercial webcam was introduced in 1994 by the US company Connectix. Only available for Apple Macintosh computers, the QuickCam was expensive and the image quality poor. Crucially, other than a variably full coffee pot, there was not much to look at.

As with many Web technologies, interest was eventually fuelled by a semi-naked woman (see **Pornography**). In 1996, Jennifer Rigley switched on JenniCam, an uncensored window to her bedroom. At her peak, Jenni was receiving 4 million visits a day. A flurry of webcam girls followed. Ten years later, Justin Kan took this to its logical conclusion, launching Justin.tv, a 24x7 webcast of his daily life from a head-mounted camera.

Today, webcams are an integral piece of our Web-browsing experience. Applications like Skype are the communication tools of choice for many. Augmented-reality applications use them to enhance the physical world. We even use them to see what our pets get up to when we're at work.

As the Web and the physical world converge, the role of the webcam becomes more central to our online experience, so much so that the next generation of webcams are likely to be wearable. Popularized by Google Glass, soon lifecasting will be just life. ∎

Images from the Cambridge students' Coffee Cam.

‘Who'd have predicted that the first
Web celebrity would be a coffee pot?’

Best viewed with ...

WEB STANDARDS

Web standards are the technical specifications recommended by the World Wide Web Consortium (W3C). Their purpose is to increase the accessibility, usability and interoperability of the Web.

An Event Apart is a conference that promotes standards-based web design.

A website complying with web standards uses accessible HTML, CSS and JavaScript. Full compliance also covers such attributes as character sets, RSS feeds, metadata, XML and the embedding of objects and scripts.

Since 2004, to comply fully with web standards, HTML should also follow semantic guidelines. This means complying with the W3C Resource Description Framework (RDF), the standard for data interchange across the Web. RDF facilitates the merging of data, even if the structure of that data differs. The framework enhances web links beyond blind signposts, to describe the relationship between linked items.

By contrast with proprietary languages, web standards are open. They can be implemented on a broad range of platforms and devices. As stated on the W3C website, web standards are designed 'to deliver the greatest benefits to the greatest number of web users while ensuring the long-term viability of any document published on the Web.'

This might seem non-controversial. Today, with a few notable exceptions, web standards are widely adopted. However, this has not always been the case. In 1998, the browser wars were at their peak (see **Web Browser**). In an effort to differentiate themselves, Netscape and Microsoft's browsers were diverging from their common roots, each creating bespoke elements of HTML. Release by release, they were becoming less compatible. Website owners found themselves having to make two versions of every site, and developers had to learn two sets of protocols.

In response, three high-profile web personalities – Glenn Davis, George Olsen and Jeffrey Zeldman – formed the Web Standards Project (WaSP). Its purpose was to campaign for common standards across browsers. As their mission statement declared, 'Support of existing W3C standards has been sacrificed in the name of innovation,

needlessly fragmenting the Web and helping no one. Our goal is to support these core standards and encourage browser makers to do the same, thereby ensuring simple, affordable access to Web technologies for all.' They were largely successful. By 2001, the leading browsers were on their way to compliance. WaSP then shifted its focus to improving the compliance of code created by authoring tools such as Dreamweaver. In 2006, its job done, WaSP disbanded.

Thanks to the tenacity of W3C and WaSP, Tim Berners-Lee's vision of the Web as an open, universal space is largely the reality. Happily, 'Best viewed with ...' is a thing of the past. ■

Portrait of Jeffrey Zeldman, founder of the email newsletter A List Apart and co-founder of the Web Standards Project (WaSP).

GeoCities screenshots captured from Olia Lialina and Dragan Espenschied's Tumblr 'One Terabyte of Kilobyte Age'.

Innovate or die

GEOCITIES

Before Facebook, before MySpace, before Friendster, there was GeoCities.

Founded in 1994, Beverly Hills Internet was a web-hosting business based in California. In mid-1995, it offered customers with no knowledge of HTML the ability to create homepages. Called 'Homesteaders', users could choose to set up their homepage within one of six neighbourhoods: the Colosseum for sports sites, Hollywood for entertainment sites, RodeoDrive for shopping, SunsetStrip for music, WallStreet for business and WestHollywood for the Gay and Lesbian community. Your neighbourhood became part of your web address – for example, www.geocities.com/Hollywood/123.

This free service was immediately popular. Chat, bulletin boards and other community elements were added. By the end of 1995, thousands of Homesteaders were setting up websites every day. The founders decided to drop their hosting business and focus on the growing community. They renamed it GeoPages, later changing it to GeoCities.

Over the next few years, new neighbourhoods, paid services and advertising were added. By the end of 1999, GeoCities was the third most visited site on the Web. Yahoo! saw an opportunity to add community elements to its offer and bought the company for $3.5 billion.

Despite the popularity of the site, GeoCities ran at a loss. Yahoo! introduced paid-for hosting and capped free accounts at 3GB of traffic per month. Unsurprisingly, Homesteaders left in bulk to try out new self-publishing platforms, like LiveJournal. The emergence of social networks, such as MySpace and Facebook, were the final nail in the coffin. In 2009, GeoCities shut down.

'Innovate or die' is an often-heard phrase in the computer industry. GeoCities proved it to be true. Between 1995 and 2009, 40 million homepages were built on GeoCities. Its template-driven homepages could be created in minutes. With hosting, FTP and URLs all built in, it was a one-stop shop for non-technical people to get on the Web. Ultimately, Wordpress and Facebook copied this model and did it better. GeoCities died from neglect.

The tools may have changed but our desire for self-expression has not. The designs were lurid and the content banal, but GeoCities introduced self-publishing to the masses, and provided the training ground for many of the first generation of bloggers. Without it, the Web would have been a less interesting place. ■

'Have you ever clicked your mouse right here? You will.'

THE BANNER AD

On 27 October 1994, HotWired.com launched the first banner ad. It was for AT&T and asked, 'Have you ever clicked your mouse right here? You will.'

They were right. Suddenly, the Web had a business model. Not only that, for the first time in its 50-year history, advertising was measurable. This fuelled a media buying frenzy. HotWired.com soon had more employees than its printed counterpart, WIRED magazine, and was earning millions of dollars a month in advertising revenue.

Newspapers and magazines were early adopters of this new form of advertising. Translating print ads into web banners was good business. Brands followed suit and poured advertising budgets into banner ads. Realizing that banners were clickable, they poured money into websites, too. Suddenly, there was an incentive to be online. The dot-com bubble had started to inflate.

However, the novelty of banners soon began to wear off. Click-through rates, once well over 10 per cent, fell to less than 1 per cent. The industry started to innovate – and not for the better. Animated banners, floating banners, expandable banners, page take-overs, pop-ups and pop-unders soon polluted the Web.

By 1997 the online advertising industry was well established. Ad-serving platforms like DoubleClick offered sophisticated targeting. By dropping **cookies** on people's computers they tracked which websites they were visiting and served banners accordingly – a contentious tactic that still causes controversy today.

The next innovation was real-time bidding (RTB). Instead of reserving prepaid advertising space on pages, advertisers bid for each impression as it is served. Information on the individual user, including their location, the software they are using and their browser history, determines how much brands will pay. Browsing from a smartphone in central London will hence result in a different banner from the one served from someone visiting the same site on an older PC in Kansas.

Social networks are now the promised land for advertising. Not only do we willingly provide our personal data, but also we declare who our friends are, and they provide their personal data too. Social networks know which brands we like, what we click on, what we share. They know where we work, rest and play. They know where we eat, sleep and drink. They know more about us than we know about ourselves, and serve up targeted ads accordingly.

The banner ad gets a bad press, and rightly so. That said, it is the reason many websites are free, and nobody is grumbling about that. ∎

Have you ever clicked your mouse right HERE? YOU WILL

The first banner ad, created by Craig Kanarick for AT&T in 1994 as part of its 'You Will' campaign.

‘Suddenly, the Web
had a business model.’

The Million Dollar Homepage, created by Alex Tew in 2005, consists of a million pixels, arranged in a 1000 × 1000 pixel grid. Advertising space on the page was sold for $1 per pixel in 100-pixel blocks.

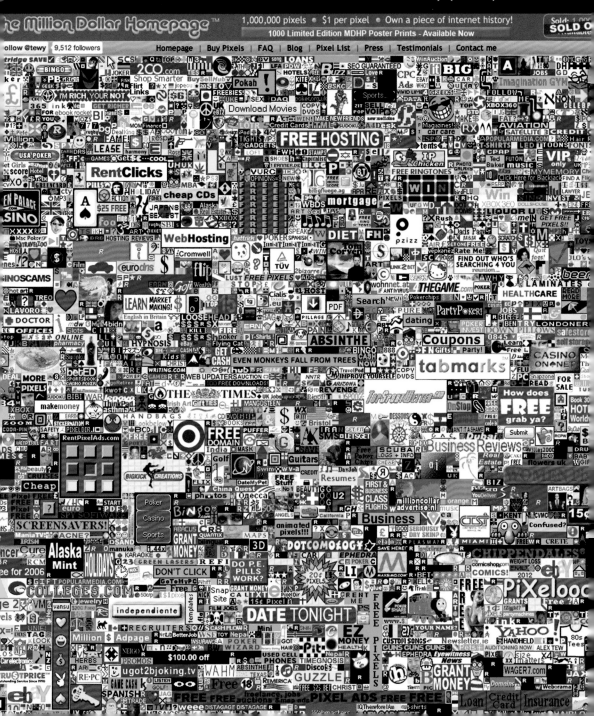

The democratization of the marketplace

IDEA № 38
WEB AUCTION

There are a handful of websites that define Web culture. eBay is one of them. The peer-to-peer auction site embodies the spirit of the Web, but, more than that, it represents a shift in global consumerism.

In September 1995, Pierre Omidyar launched AuctionWeb, the first incarnation of eBay. When a broken laser pointer was bought for $14.83, Omidyar contacted the buyer to make sure he knew it didn't work. The buyer explained, 'I'm a collector of broken laser pointers'. Omidyar realized that given a large enough audience, there was a buyer for almost anything.

Omidyar moved the site from his personal account to its own domain and started charging sellers commission. In 1996, the site hosted 250,000 auctions. The following year, AuctionWeb hosted 2 million auctions in January alone. The online marketplace was drawing a crowd.

In September 1997, Omidyar decided to change the domain name to echobay.com, after his consulting firm Echo Bay Technology Group. The domain already existed, so he shortened it to eBay. It was a smart move. Within ten years, the site had hundreds of millions of registered users and revenues in excess of $7 billion.

Part of the appeal of eBay, other than its catchy name, is its bidding system. It operates an auction-style called Proxy Bidding. The bidder's highest bid is sealed. The winner pays the second-highest bid, plus an increment. It's similar to the Vickrey Auction used by stamp collectors since 1893. In this style of auction, the highest bidder wins but pays the price of the second-highest bid. It gives bidders an incentive to bid their true price.

There are, of course, a number of stories that have entered into eBay folklore, from the ten-year-old toasted sandwich that bore the image of the Virgin Mary, to naming rights of an unborn child. These tales demonstrate that Omidyar's hunch was right. Almost anything can be bought and sold. Anyone can sell to anybody.

Thanks to the Web's biggest marketplace, buyers are no longer at the mercy of a handful of powerful retailers. Prices and products can be compared to such an extent that fairness and honesty are eBay's greatest assets. The availability of more complete information and low barriers to entry provides an almost perfect market. A perfect market where you can buy a broken laser pointer, should you so wish. ■

'Fairness and honesty are eBay's greatest assets.'

Broken laser pointers, Britney Spears' chewing gum, a sprout and a toasted sandwich bearing the image of the Virgin Mary – just a few of the strange items that have been put up for sale on eBay.

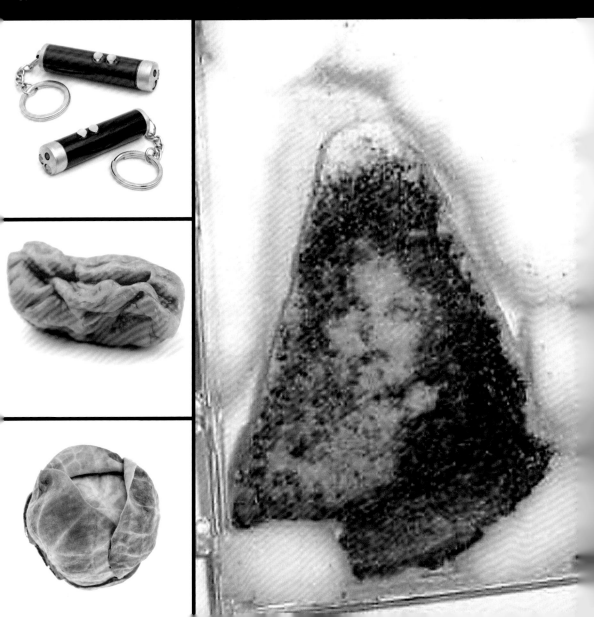

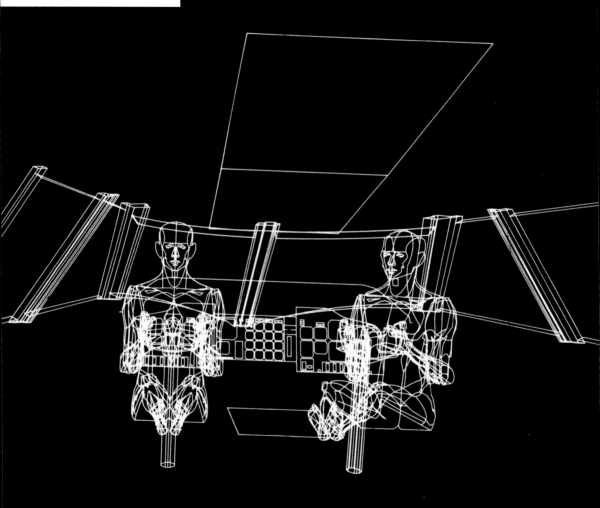

William Fetter's Boeing Man was used to design a virtual cockpit ergonomically. The manufacturing and design industries have put people at the centre of design ever since.

Don't make me think

USER-CENTRED DESIGN

Websites are often designed from a technical or business perspective. Usability is an afterthought. User-centred design (UCD) optimizes an interface or product around the person who is going to be using it.

The father of user-centred design is arguably William Fetter, an American designer who worked for Boeing. In 1960 he coined the term Computer Graphics. In 1964, he made the first computer model of a human body. Known as 'Boeing Man', this wireframe pilot was used to design a virtual cockpit ergonomically, optimizing his ability to reach the instruments. The manufacturing and design industries have put people at the centre of design ever since.

When the webpage emerged, design was not a factor. It was a simple text document with embedded hyperlinks. The only design consideration was font size. Spoilt by a decade of desktop publishing, graphic designers shunned the limited possibilities of HTML. Engineers and computer programmers controlled the space. Webpages were information-led. Form was functional. As the Web developed into a graphical environment, layout became an issue.

By the late 90s it was chaos. Images, animated GIFs, Flash and Java applets competed for space within frames and tables. This new media was crying out for new rules. Step forward Jakob Nielsen, engineer and usability expert at Sun Microsystems.

In 1995, Nielsen launched his website useit.com. While his views were controversial, especially among Web designers trying to push back the boundaries of HTML, his ideas were a beacon in the emerging field of Web usability. He advocated user testing and paper prototypes that put the user's expectations at the centre of the design process. He was a champion of minimal designs that spoke the language of the user. This meant following real-world conventions and avoiding system-orientated terminology and functionality. Don Norman, Jakob Nielsen's business partner, describes it well: 'We must design our technologies for the way people actually behave, not the way we would like them to.'

Steve Krug's ideas on usability are less contentious. His seminal book from 2000 says everything you need to know about user-centred design: *Don't Make Me Think.* ∎

Don Norman, co-founder of the Nielsen Norman Group and author of The Design of Everyday Things.

We are all Net Artists now

IDEA № 40

NET ART

In 1952, computer scientist Christopher Strachey developed a program for the Manchester Mark 1 computer that created randomized love letters. It was the first example of computer art.

With Strachey's generative love letters, the result is secondary to the process. This typifies computer art and the Net Art movement that followed. Unexpected outcomes are welcome, opening doors rather than closing them. Even the way the genre got its name was serendipitous: ASCII artist

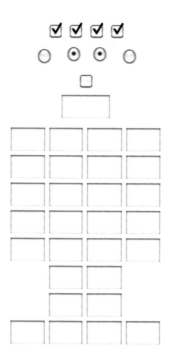

Vuk Cosic received a corrupted email in 1995; the only words he could make out were 'Net Art'.

Born in Belgrade, Cosic emigrated to Slovenia in the early 90s. While US dot-com companies seized on the commercial potential of the Web, Eastern Europe was critical to its artistic development. The break-up of the Soviet Union created an optimistic, open atmosphere, exemplified by the Web. Russian artists Olia Lialina and Alexei Shulgin were hugely influential. Lialina's *My Boyfriend Came Back From The War*, from 1996, is a hypertext narrative, as envisioned by the godfather of hyertext, Vannevar Bush, at the end of World War II (see **Hypertext**). Shulgin's *Form Art* manipulates HTML's layout capabilities, using checkboxes, radio buttons and text fields to create forms. The appearance varies from browser to browser, evolving with every release, as if it were alive.

Many of the early online art projects addressed technology as the subject matter, as well as the medium. Heath Bunting's *King's Cross Phone-In* (1994) demonstrated the power of network technology. Bunting listed the telephone numbers of the public phones at London's King's Cross station on his website and encouraged visitors to call the numbers at a certain time, or to show up and speak to a stranger. In

1995, Joan Heemskerk and Dirk Paesmans, known as Jodi, created wwwwwwwww.jodi.org, a website highlighting the hidden depths of the Web. The site appears to be indecipherable – only when the visitor views the source code can they see the true message. The HTML takes the form of an atomic bomb.

Another recurring theme in Net Art is the commercialization of the Web. Webby Award-winner and 'the first Internet application designed by artists' the Web Stalker is an experimental browser. Developed by British Web Art activists I/O/D in 1997, the browser strips out the superfluous, so only the raw text, links and metadata remain.

The Web gave artists who operated outside the traditional art world access to a global audience. Free from the commercial world of galleries and art-world institutions, Net Art was a reaction against the cultural elite, its lack of marketability making it all the more authentic.

Artists and designers like Aram Bartoll, Aaron Koblin and Rafäel Rozendaal continue the spirit of Net Art, but things have changed. Net Art is no longer about internet culture it's about the huge impact of the internet on culture. With the growth of the social Web, the genre has slipped quietly into the shadows. We are all Net Artists now. ■

ABOVE: Hybridmoment.com by the prolific net artist Rafaël Rozendaal.

OPPOSITE: An example of Alexei Shulgin's Form Art, which displays differently across browsers and evolves with them.

Error 404: Page Not Found

IDEA № 41
DIGITAL FRAGILITY

Brewster Kahle, founder of the Internet Archive and advocate of universal access to knowledge.

Printed in 1455, 48 copies of the Gutenberg Bible exist, yet not one copy of a website made a little over 20 years ago survives.

The Web is a little over two decades old, but it has transformed our lives. We do almost everything differently. Tragically, over this short time, technological change has been so fast that early websites disappeared almost as soon as they appeared. The first webpage was published in August 1991 (see **The Project**). Its story is typical, being continually overwritten until March 1992. No copy of the original webpage, not even a screenshot, exists. The record of that monumental point in history has been lost forever.

This is not an isolated case. Forty thousand homepages were lost when Yahoo! deleted **Geocities** in 2009 and it is estimated that more than 0.2 per cent of the Web disappears every day.

Digital content is so easy to duplicate that copies are not valued. Worse, the original version is also often considered disposable. Combine this with the rapid obsolescence of digital storage formats, and it is easy to see why many experts describe the early years of the Web as a digital dark age.

The Internet Archive (archive.org) was established to fight this trend. Accessible via the Wayback Machine – named after the time machine in the TV series *Rocky & Bullwinkle* – the service has been archiving websites since October 1996. Founded by Brewster Kahle, it is a hugely valuable resource but it is also an imperfect one: the first five years of the Web are not archived; some website owners choose to exclude their sites; other websites suffer from missing media and broken links.

The last 20 years have seen the birth and rise of the Web at an astronomical pace. We have witnessed the birth of the Information Age, equal in magnitude to the transition to the modern world from the Middle Ages. We have a responsibility to expose this artistic, commercial and social digital history – the building blocks of modern culture – to future generations, an audience who will be unable to imagine a world without the Web.

Until we discover the digital equivalent of acid-free paper, bits and bytes remain extremely fragile. ∎

The author's Error 404
exhibition showcases websites
from the pre-social Web
and promotes digital
preservation.

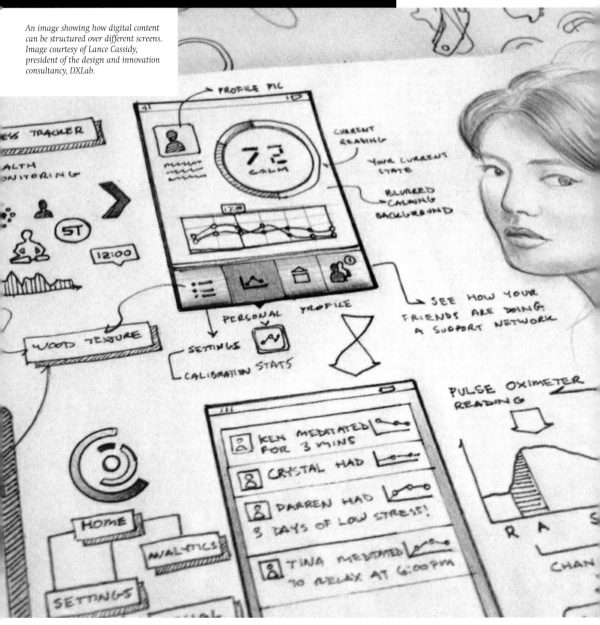

An image showing how digital content can be structured over different screens. Image courtesy of Lance Cassidy, president of the design and innovation consultancy, DXLab.

Fail to plan, plan to fail

INFORMATION ARCHITECTURE

Information architecture (IA) is the art and science of organizing and structuring a website. The discipline combines interaction design, usability, search and labelling to make information as easy as possible to find and consume.

IA is closely related to information design, the practice of presenting information in a way that enables quick and easy understanding.

The term 'information architecture' was coined in 1976 by Richard Saul Wurman, an American architect and graphic designer. He wanted to draw a distinction between aesthetics and systems. Information architecture refers to how efficiently a system performs, rather than how it looks. Wurman's work was an attempt to impose order on the huge amount of information generated by modern society. As he put it, 'The explosion of data needed an architecture, needed a series of systems, needed systemic design.'

In the late 90s, Wurman's vision was embraced by web designers. As websites became increasingly complex, specialist roles emerged and audience expectations rose. There was a clear need for a joined-up planning process. Technical specification documents were too inaccessible, sketches too superficial and prototypes too expensive. The solution followed that of the construction industry; just as a successful building starts with an architectural plan, so does a successful website.

When someone first visits a website, they assess relationships between topics and make guesses about where to find things. Information architecture aims to deliver consistent methods of grouping, ordering, labelling and graphically arranging information. This allows users to extend their knowledge from pages they have visited to pages they are unfamiliar with.

The key outputs of the information architecture phase of designing a website consists of a sitemap, navigation system, wireframes, user journeys and functionality diagrams. A sitemap specifies the extent of the website. Navigation describes how information will be grouped. Wireframes detail the structure and content of each page. User journeys demonstrate how a visitor might move around a website. Functionality diagrams provide additional detail as required. Unlike a written specification, these visual checklists can be quickly and consistently understood by all parties. Once the underlying structure of information is agreed, designers, developers, content creators and site owners can commence their specialist tasks with confidence.

Information architecture is a fundamental part of the web-design process. Visitors expect content to be arranged in a rational and logical way. Failure to do so results in frustration, fewer page visits and ultimately fewer site visitors. As the old saying goes, 'Fail to plan, plan to fail'. ∎

Anyone wanna erk?

WEB CHAT

Talkomatic, the first online chat system, was created at the University of Illinois in 1973. Five users could chat concurrently, their messages appearing character by character as they were typed.

The social web did not start with Facebook in 2005 or even classmates.com in 1995. The Web has always been social. Ever since we connected two computers, the first thing people wanted to do was talk to one another.

The first online chat system was called Talkomatic. Created at the University of Illinois in 1973 as part of a computerized learning system, it allowed messages to appear magically on users' screens, character by character, as they were typed. It was an instant hit.

The first dedicated online chat service was CompuServe's CB Simulator. Named after Citizens Band radio, it quickly became CompuServe's most popular service. As on Talkomatic before it, the most popular activity was flirting. One thing led to another and on Valentine's Day 1983, the first online wedding took place. Debbie Fuhrman, George Stickles and a minister logged on to different computers in the same room in Texas and tied the knot in front of 100 other CompuServe members.

The most common chat standard used today is Internet Relay Chat (IRC), developed in 1988 by Finnish student Jarkko Oikarinen at the University of Oulu. Like the best products and services, IRC spread virally. Oikarinen got his friends at Denver and Oregon universities to create IRC servers so they could chat too. They got their friends to do the same. There were soon thousands of installations of the software around the world. Everybody wanted to 'erk'.

In 1995, Sun Microsystems released Java, which enabled the dynamic exchange of data over the Net. Java applets incorporating news tickers, live weather reports and WYSIWYG editors popped up across websites, but the most popular applications by far were chat rooms.

When entering a chat room, the first thing you were likely to be asked was 'A/S/L?', meaning Age, Sex and Location. In a chat room, these were flexible attributes. In one room, you could be an 18-year-old model from Paris, in the next, an ageing South American rock star. In fact, most people were school kids, running up huge bills and hogging the phone line. 'Get off the internet, I want to make a call' was a commonly heard expression in the '90s.

The newest wave of chat software combines Voice over IP (VoIP), video conferencing and chat, the most popular of which is Skype. Released in 2003 by the people who created the peer-to-peer file-sharing software Kazaa, Skype now has over 600 million users. Whether it is face to face, in chat rooms or over video conferencing, one thing is clear. People like to talk. ∎

'In one room, you could be an 18-year-old model from Paris, in the next, an ageing South American rock star.'

'Style is a simple way of saying complicated things'

IDEA № 44

CASCADING STYLE SHEETS

The French poet Jean Cocteau once said, 'Style is a simple way of saying complicated things'. He was not talking about Cascading Style Sheets, but he might as well have been.

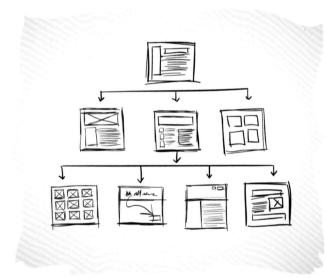

Cascading Style Sheets allow a document's style to be influenced by multiple style sheets. One style sheet can inherit or 'cascade' from another, permitting a mixture of stylistic preferences.

Cascading Style Sheets (CSS) control presentational elements such as layout, colours and fonts. This was not always the case. In the early days of the Web, each page was assembled by an independent chunk of HTML, and layout options were limited. Fonts and colours could not be manipulated. An email sent to the W3C mailing list in 1994 is revealing: 'It has been a constant source of delight for me over the past

year to get to continually tell hordes (literally) of people who want to – strap yourselves in, here it comes – control what their documents look like in ways that would be trivial in TeX, Microsoft Word, and every other common text processing environment: "Sorry, you're screwed."' The author of the message was Marc Andreessen, the creator of the Mosaic browser.

As the Web reached a more mainstream audience, designers started to demand greater control over the appearance of a page. Despite the protestations of people like Andreessen, they got what they wished for. The cost was more complex HTML. It was more difficult to code, labour-intensive to maintain and slow to load.

Style sheets were suggested as the solution. This was not a new idea. When the Web was first conceived, Robert Cailliau saw the need for three types of style sheet: one for editing, one for presentation and one for printing. Style sheets were also consistent with accepted wisdom, that structure should be separated from presentation, an idea first expressed by the father of **markup language**, William Tunnicliffe.

Two existing style-sheet solutions were combined to form the foundation of what would become CSS. Cascading

'Sites that use style sheets are easier to build, faster to load and ensure consistency across navigation and design'

Håkon Wium Lie, Opera's Chief Technology Officer and co-creator of the CSS standard.

HTML Style Sheets (CHSS), as used by the Opera browser, and Bert Bos's Stylesheet Proposal. Opera's Chief Technology Officer, Håkon Wium Lie, and Bos worked together to create the W3C specification. By the end of 1996 they had completed the task.

It was almost four years before any major Web **browser** implemented CSS. Under pressure from the Web Standards Project (WaSP), Internet Explorer 5.0 – released in March 2000 – was almost fully CSS compliant. By the end of 2001, Netscape Navigator had followed suit.

CSS reinvented web design. Sites that use style sheets are easier to build and maintain. The more compact code is faster to load and easier for search engines to index. Finally, CSS ensure consistency across navigation and design, making for a better user experience.

Style is substance, after all. ■

'Data that describes data'

METADATA

There are more than 4 billion pages on the Web. Estimates have suggested that if you were to print them, they would take 57,000 years to read.

Not everybody wants to read the entire Web. Luckily, we have ways of prioritizing what we read. It's called metadata.

Metadata is data that describes data. For example, how it was created, when it was created, who created it, etc. An early example of metadata is the Dewey Decimal System used by libraries: 3 x 5-inch cards are used to display a book's title, author, subject matter and an alphanumeric code indicating the physical location of the book within the library.

Metadata is now pervasive. Every digital object is, or at least can be, described in some way. The clever thing is, it carries its own description with it. Metadata describing a digital photograph may include information such as the resolution of the picture, its colour depth, when it was created, the type of camera that was used to take it, and copyright information. Metadata describing a text file may contain the length of the document, the author and when it was written. Metadata about a web page will include a title, describe the content, list keywords, supply copyright information, etc.

Title and Description tags are most commonly used. The Title tag appears in the top bar of the browser; the Description tag is hidden in the source code. Search engines also use these tags in their listings. The Title tag is the active link you click on, and the Description tag is the snippet of information below. While these do not affect search results, they can influence click-through rates.

The Keyword tag was popular in the mid-90s. Search engines, such as AltaVista, used them to determine rankings. However, by the late '90s the minority had spoilt it for everyone else by creating unreliable and misleading keywords.

In 1999, the W3C released the Resource Description Framework (RDF), an evolution of the metadata model. RDF is a step towards the Semantic Web, structuring unstructured data so that it can be identified and merged (see also **The Semantic Web**).

The Web contains an unimaginable amount of information. Metadata gives us half a chance of finding that picture of a kitten we really want. ∎

Henriette Avram, creator of the first digital metadata in 1970, the MARC standards (Machine-readable Cataloging standards) at the Library of Congress.

'Metadata gives us half a chance of finding that picture of a kitten we really want.'

NGC 1432 / Maia nebula -

astrometry.net

Astrometry.net is building an engine that automatically adds astrometric metadata to any astronomical image. The result will be the most comprehensive image of the night sky the world has ever known.

Tom Conrad from Pandora speaks onstage during the 15th Annual Webby Awards at the Hammerstein Ballroom in New York City, 13 June 2011.

The Oscars of online media

IDEA № 46

THE WEBBY AWARDS

From the very early days of the Web, no institution has done more to promote excellence in interaction design than the Webby Awards.

The success of the Webbys parallels that of the media they celebrate. When the awards were launched in 1995, approximately 100 million people were browsing the World Wide Web. In 2014, the figure exceeds 2.5 billion. The awards now include more than 140 categories, across web design, interactive advertising, online film and mobile applications. Along the way there have been world-changing ideas, star-studded ceremonies and some memorable five-word speeches (the word limit for acceptance speeches).

The name most synonymous with the Webbys is Tiffany Shlain, who launched the awards in 1995. Shlain brought in major sponsors, including Intel and Audi, and secured big-name guests such as Al Gore and Prince. The ceremony quickly shifted from 600- to 3,000-seater venues; from Bimbo's nightclub in San Francisco to the Hammerstein Ballroom in New York.

Unlike the Oscars, anyone who submits an entry form can be shortlisted for a Webby. Nominees are then chosen by the International Academy of Digital Arts and Sciences (IADAS), a global organization of industry experts. Members include Arianna Huffington, Editor-in-Chief of the *Huffington Post*, *Simpsons* creator Matt Groening, Twitter co-founder Biz Stone and Tumblr founder David Karp.

Those fortunate to have been honoured over the years include well-known names such as Google, *Wired*, ESPN, Nike, Netflix and Björk, as well as emerging forces such as Songify and change.org. And let's not forget Bianca's Smut Shack, best sex site, from the Webbys' more irreverent '90s era.

Now approaching their twentieth year, the Webby Awards are more popular than ever, receiving more than 10,000 entries from over 60 countries. Chief Executive David-Michel Davies puts this success down to the Webbys' ability to keep pace with the fast-changing nature of the Web. 'When new parts of the internet emerge, like a burgeoning online film and video industry in 2007, we are quick to respond with new categories to honour all the new places the internet takes us.'

This is undoubtedly true, but what really pulls in the crowds are the cleverly crafted five-word speeches. When Anna Wintour picked up the Best Fashion Website award for *Vogue*, she quipped 'Sometimes ... geeks can be chic'. Greenpeace's speech resonated with the web generation when they declared, 'There's nothing good on TV'. But perhaps the most fitting speech has come from Vinton Cerf when he received a lifetime achievement award: 'You ain't seen nothing yet.'

Webby Awards, we salute you. ∎

The Webby Award trophy represents a spiral of creative DNA, definitely not a mattress spring.

Money talks

PAY PER CLICK

In February 1998, Jeffrey Brewer changed the advertising industry forever. He introduced the world to pay per click.

Pay per click (PPC) is a model in which advertisers pay a website owner only when their ad is clicked on. It eliminates the uncertainty of pay-per-impression (PPM) models, where the advertiser pays each time the ad is displayed, regardless of whether the viewer takes any action.

Although the model is now synonymous with AdWords, Google was slow to adopt PPC. AltaVista, Excite and Yahoo! got there first, adopting Brewer's goto.com platform in the late '90s.

Google has always displayed sponsored links next to natural search results, but it originally operated a pay-per-impression model. As with **banner ads**, advertisers paid per thousand views. Google AdWords launched in 2000, and with it Google adopted pay per click. It was a straight copy of the goto.com platform with one small adjustment. Instead of ranking advertisements by bid price alone, they took into account the click-through rate. Those that are clicked on more rise to the top, encouraging quality and maximizing Google's profits. Advertisers loved it. Searchers welcomed it. Google built an empire on it.

Pay per click shows no sign of slowing down – the model Brewer developed dominates online marketing.

Pay-per-click advertising generated revenues of $42 billion for Google alone in 2012. That is a lot of clicks. The billions Google earns from AdWords not only fund its natural search business but also allow it to invest in its cloud-based services, such as Gmail, Google Maps and Google Docs – the services that shaped Web 2.0.

Sponsored links have undoubtedly shaped the Web, but does offering a shortcut to the first page of Google search results undermine the integrity of the Web? As more and more brands join the feeding frenzy, Google and other search engines further degrade their own *raison d'être*. Perhaps pay-per-click inflation will encourage brands to rethink their approach to online marketing, but while they can pay Google to look the other way, I doubt it. ∎

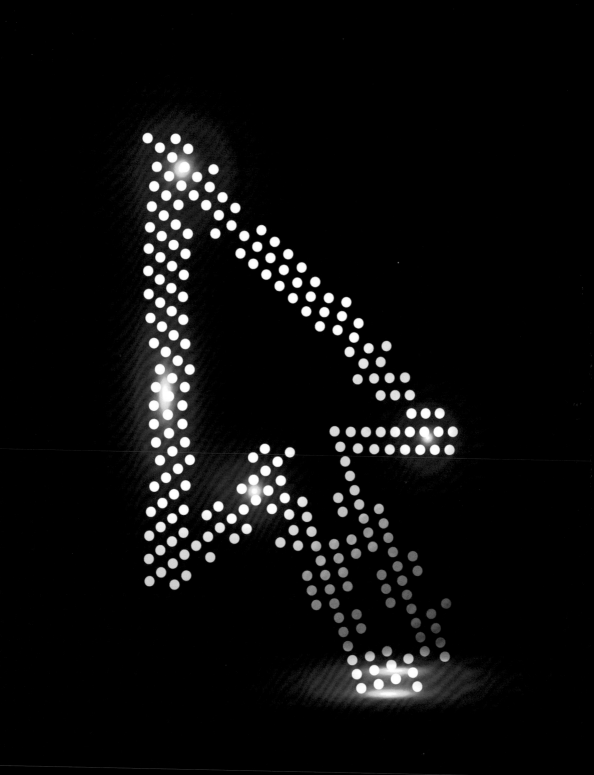

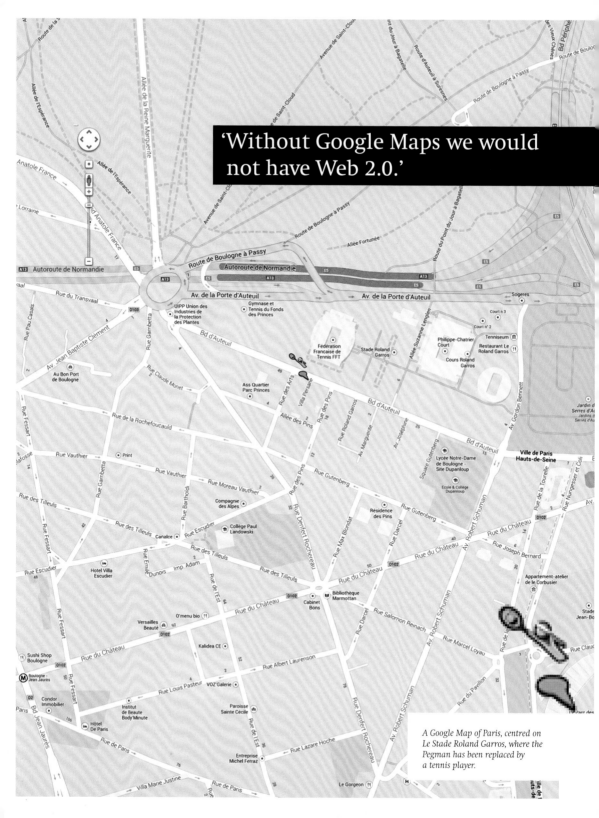

'Without Google Maps we would not have Web 2.0.'

A Google Map of Paris, centred on Le Stade Roland Garros, where the Pegman has been replaced by a tennis player.

Plotting the Web's future

WEB MAPPING

Where maps were static, now they are dynamic. Where before we turned the page of an atlas, now we pan and zoom our way around a screen.

The first interactive map was developed in 1993 by Steve Putz at Xerox PARC. The Interactive Map Viewer automatically generated GIF images based on parameters encoded in the URL. It was an early demonstration of interactive information retrieval on the Web.

In 1994, at the University of Minnesota, the researcher Stephen Lime created UMN MapServer, a Web-based tool for exploring a million acres of wilderness on the Canadian border. The area was under the administration of the US Forestry Service, which saw the potential of Lime's tool to plot global forestry information. After securing funding from NASA and the European Union, UMN MapServer became the first platform for the remote accessing of satellite imagery. Job done, Lime and the University of Minnesota made MapServer open source. The map-generation engine is used to this day to track hurricanes, plot shipping routes and plan bicycle trips.

The first commercial Web map was developed by the Chicago-based company R. R. Donnelley & Sons, who had been making roadmaps since the 1960s. Its online route-finding software, MapQuest, launched on 5 February 1996. Direction finding would never be the same again. The same data used to power MapQuest now powers Google Maps.

Perhaps one of the biggest success stories in the world of Web mapping is OpenStreetMap. It was developed in 2004 by Steve Coast, whose aim was to create Wikipedia for maps. He was convinced that a crowdsourced geographic database would be a useful way to keep maps up to date. He was right. Since its inception, OpenStreetMap has benefited from over 300,000 contributors and has been adopted by Apple, Craigslist, Flickr and Foursquare.

The Web map of choice for millions of users is Google Maps. It began life as an offline program designed by two Danish brothers, Lars and Jens Rasmussen, and the Web-based version launched in October 2004. The impact of Google Maps goes far beyond online mapping. Its use of Asynchronous JavaScript and XML (**AJAX**) created a seamless experience that inspired the next generation of websites. Without Google Maps, we would not have Web 2.0.

Thanks to pioneers like the UMN MapServer, MapQuest and OpenStreetMap, maps are no longer about geographical landscapes, they are about data. Every day, they become more comprehensive, more accurate and more useful. And this process of adding detail will never stop. Maps will become increasingly realistic, but perhaps more intriguingly, reality will become more like a map. ■

IDEA Nº 49

BLOGGING

In 1994, Dave Winer started DaveNet, an email newsletter that discussed the latest developments in the computer industry. Frustrated with the lack of coverage his software company received in the trade press, Winer saw DaveNet as an opportunity to bypass mainstream media.

The infamous blog 'Diary of a London Call Girl' was voted Blog of the Year by The Guardian *newspaper in 2003 and spawned the book* The Intimate Adventures of a London Call Girl.

Belle de Jour

The Intimate Adventures of a London Call Girl

The flagship product of Winer's company was Frontier, an early scripting language for the Mac. By 1996 it had evolved into software for the creation of websites. Winer used it to create and manage his own website – Scripting News – which continued where DaveNet left off.

Winer's daily updates attracted an audience of like-minded people. One of these people was Jorn Barger, who adopted Frontier to manage his own website, Robot Wisdom. In December 1997, Barger began posting daily entries on his website and started referring to it as a 'web log'. His prolific postings, on everything from artificial intelligence to Kate Bush, gained global attention. It was not long before the term web log was adopted by other people to describe their daily musings. In 1999, Peter Merholz jokingly wrote it as 'we blog' on his website. Regularly updated web journals have been known as 'blogs' ever since.

Early blogs were simply regularly updated websites. The emergence of specific blogging platforms, such as Blogger, Open Diary and LiveJournal, standardized the format. Articles are usually posted in reverse chronological order, visitors are able to leave

'Sites like Scripting News and Robot Wisdom were trailblazers for what we now refer to as social media'

Lina Ben Mhenni's blog, A Tunisian Girl, documented the Tunisian Revolution and continues to speak out against political corruption in Tunisia.

comments, and links to other blogs are encouraged.

Blogs are written by people from all walks of life, from politicians to call girls. Whatever the subject, informal, peer-produced content now sits alongside professional journalism. Consumers have become producers. With that comes a shift in the balance of power. Governments, brands and the media have to forge more equitable relationships with their audiences. Increased choice and variety of views can only be a good thing.

Blogging has reinvented a media landscape previously dominated by the mass-media broadcast industry. People now have more sources from which to obtain their news. Sites like Scripting News and Robot Wisdom were trailblazers for citizen journalism, self-publishing and pretty much everything else we now refer to as social media. They have been instrumental in helping the Web become the participatory medium it was always envisioned to be. And hallelujah to that. ∎

The home page of the Tunisian Girl blog.

Saviour of the animated universe

SCALEABLE VECTOR GRAPHICS

In 1997, users were upgrading from 28k to 33k modems. The information superhighway was far from super. In June, Macromedia released Flash – its vector graphic-driven files loaded ten times faster than HTML, with ten times the impact. The online experience was improved a hundredfold. Suddenly the Web looked like TV.

In January 1993, Jonathan Gay, Charlie Jackson and Michelle Welsh founded FutureWave Software. Their vision was to create a software application that allowed people to bypass the mouse and draw directly on a computer screen. They called it SmartSketch, but just as it was about to launch, AT&T scrapped PenPoint, the operating system it was built on. FutureWave had no choice but to adapt its software to the keyboard and mouse. From having a market to itself, it was suddenly competing with Adobe Illustrator and Macromedia FreeHand. SmartSketch had become a 'me too' product.

With the crazy idea that it might be possible to put animations on the Web, Gay and his programming sidekick, Robert Tatsumi, started to focus on SmartSketch's animation capabilities. In 1994, the only way to do this was through Java. The results were painfully slow, but they stuck with it. The breakthrough came the following year, with the release of Netscape Navigator 2.0. This second version of the Netscape **browser** added a whole load of features, including Netscape Mail, JavaScript, support for animated GIFs and, crucially, an API (application programming interface) for plug-ins. The ability to extend the browser via a plug-in meant that SmartSketch animations could be as fluid online as they were offline. SmartSketch was renamed FutureSplash Animator and eventually shipped in May 1996.

FutureSplash immediately caught the attention of Microsoft, which was playing catch-up with Netscape and throwing everything at it, including relaunching MSN as a web TV network. Internet Explorer 3.0, released in August 1996, shipped with the FutureSplash plug-in, and suddenly it was mass market. Disney Online quickly became a client and then Fox launched the *Simpsons* website using FutureSplash. The six-person FutureWave team was hot property. By the end of the year, FutureSplash had been purchased by Macromedia and renamed Macromedia Flash. The Design Director at Macromedia was musician David Hillman Curtis, the nephew of Chris Hillman of The Byrds. Hillman Curtis redeveloped the Macromedia website using the newly acquired software and, in doing so, created the first Flash website. A wave of non-programmers followed in his creative footsteps.

The release of Macromedia Flash was a tipping point. It opened up the Web to animators and illustrators in the same way as the Mosaic browser had done for the very first web designers four years earlier. Brands could at last see the potential of this new media, which attracted serious investment, prompting the dot-com gold rush.

Sure, there were some dodgy moments along the way, but by and large Flash has made the Web a more interesting place. ■

In 1999, Jonni Nitro was the most exciting animation on the Web. Using a highly stylized video-to-vector process, Tubatomic's animated series took its visual cues from graphic novels like Frank Miller's Sin City.

Send and thou shalt receive

IDEA № 51

WEBMAIL

'Don't tell anyone, this isn't what we're supposed to be working on', said Ray Tomlinson when he sent the first email message in 1971. He need not have worried – his SNDMSG program soon had the support of everyone else working on ARPANET.

Ten years later, an Internet Standard for electronic mail was introduced. Simple Message Transfer Protocol (SMTP) laid the foundations for the widespread adoption of email. At first, however, it was used by scientists, academics and government. It was not until 1988, when commercial traffic was given access to the internet, that email really took off.

In the early days, most people got their email addresses from their **internet service provider**. If you moved provider, you got a new email address. Like many people, Sabeer Bhatia and Jack Smith found this frustrating. Even more frustratingly, their employers firewall-blocked their AOL email addresses, which meant that when they wanted to swap documents for the web-storage software they were developing at the time – JavaSoft – they were forced to use floppy disks.

Smith pointed out that access to the Web was unrestricted. If they adapted their JavaSoft program, it would be relatively straightforward to display emails in HTML, circumventing the firewall. Not only that, if they provided email addresses as well, people would not be tied to an ISP. They decided to change JavaSoft into an email program. Originally called HTML mail, HoTMaiL launched on 4 July 1996.

Having burnt through its venture capital, Hotmail had no money for marketing. It was decided to add a link to the bottom of each outgoing message: 'Get your own Hotmail at www.hotmail.com'. Every email became an advert for the service. This early example of viral marketing had spectacular results. Within two months, it had 100,000 customers. Within six months, a million.

Hotmail followed the high-risk, 'get large or get lost' model typical of many dot-com start-ups of the time (see **The Dot-com Bubble**). The service was partially funded by banner ads, but profit was not the primary motivation. By the end of 1997, 10 million people had signed up for the free email service.

Microsoft purchased Hotmail for $400 million in December of that year – an enormous fee for a loss-making business. It marked the start of the incredible valuation of web-based businesses, and was the catalyst for the dot-com bubble.

Along with eBay, Amazon and PayPal, Hotmail is one of the few dot-com success stories. It owes its success to the universal adoption of email. Online videos, peer-to-peer networks and social media have all been touted as killer apps, but email remains the most popular online activity. The most important communications tool since the telephone, email is the essential internet service. Thanks to services like Hotmail, it is available to everyone for free. ∎

Meg Ryan in the 1998 romcom You've Got Mail, *named after the greeting that AOL users heard when they received a new email.*

We are what we share

IDEA № 52
VIRAL CONTENT

Five thousand years ago, Mesopotamians used cylinder seals to roll an impression on to wet clay. Two thousand years ago, the Chinese were using woodblock prints to reproduce images.

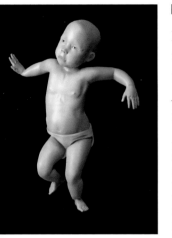

First appearing in 1996, the Dancing Baby was one of the first viral videos.

Viral content has existed as long as we have been able to replicate objects.

With the invention of the printing press, the camera and the record player, reproducing content became an industry. Viral content is now understood to be content that is shared peer to peer, bypassing traditional media channels. While there are some pre-Web examples, such as the trading of bootleg VHS copies of the cult classic film *Heavy Metal Parking Lot*, the Web has proved to be a perfect breeding ground for sharing viral content. Digital content is easy to copy, and the Web makes it easy to share.

While computer viruses are often sinister, viral content is usually harmless fun. One of the first viral phenomena was a 3D animation of a dancing baby. Appearing on our screens in 1996, the demo file was first shared across email, websites and forums before featuring on TV shows like *Ally McBeal*, *3rd Rock from the Sun* and *The Simpsons*. It was to be the first in a series of unusual dancers, including hamsters, elves and inmates of a maximum-security Filipino prison.

Savvy marketers recognize the potential of freely distributed ads. Blendtec's YouTube channel, 'Will It Blend?' – featuring its founder, Tom Dickson, blending household objects from golf balls to iPhones – has been viewed hundreds of millions of times. Obama Girl's 'I Got a Crush on Obama' was viewed millions of times during the 2008 US presidential election.

But why is some content shared and some shunned? Content that inspires an emotional response – laughter or disbelief – is a good place to start. Other than that, there seems to be no formula.

Examining why we share, rather than what we share, is perhaps more informative. As social animals, we are driven to forge and strengthen friendships. Dancing babies and hamsters make us smile. We share them to make our friends smile too. The content is not really important. It is the act of sharing and acknowledgement that is significant. Tellingly, we are even more likely to share content from a weak connection than a close friend. By sharing the content we validate the friendship.

More than this, every time we share a link, we are saying something about ourselves. We are defining who we are and who we want to be. Sharing shapes our identity. ∎

blendtec.com

*Will It Blend? is a viral marketing
campaign demonstrating the
Blendtec blender. In the viral ads,
founder Tom Dickson demonstrates
the power of the blender by blending*

Planking is the act of lying down, arms by your side, in an unusual location. Seen here, Deb Taylor of *What's Deb Doing?*

Copying is the sincerest form of flattery

IDEA № 53

INTERNET MEME

A Golden-mantled Ground Squirrel crashes the Brandt's self-portrait at Banff National Park in 2009. The image has become a popular meme, known as Crasher Squirrel.

Have you ever played an April Fool's joke? That's a meme. Have you ever worn your baseball cap back to front? That's a meme too. Have you ever said, 'Cheers'? You get the idea.

A meme is a behaviour that is transmitted from person to person. The term was coined by evolutionary biologist Richard Dawkins in his 1976 book *The Selfish Gene*, from the Greek, *mimema*, meaning 'imitate'. Examples of memes cited in the book include stories, sayings, fashions and learnt skills. Dawkins sums up a meme as 'a unit of cultural transmission', meaning just about anything you can think of is potentially a meme. It can be a phrase, image, behaviour, sound or fashion.

According to Dawkins' theory, memes evolve in the same way as living things. Some become extinct, some spread and others mutate. The meme is perhaps most simply described by Malcolm Gladwell as 'an idea that behaves like a virus that moves through a population, taking hold in each person it infects'. This is true, but it confuses a meme with viral content.

Memes differ from viral campaigns in that they evolve and change over time. Crasher Squirrel is a meme, appearing in a different photograph each time it's shared. Dancing Baby is viral; the same file is shared every time.

Historically, a meme would travel via word of mouth, usually as an interesting story, a funny joke or an expression of speech. An internet meme spreads from person to person via social networks, blogs, content aggregators, instant messages and email. Away from the keyboard, memes evolve and spread relatively slowly. On the Web, they can spread extremely rapidly, potentially reaching a global audience in hours.

Internet memes are often humorous, such as Crasher Squirrel or the Star Wars Kid. Humour reaches the most people because it is easy to forward funny content to large numbers of people. Conversational expressions are popular too, such as 'Keep Calm and ...'. Whatever the motive, in each case a piece of customized content spreads between people in a virus-like fashion.

Internet memes have attracted a lot of academic attention. Making ideas stick has enormous potential for influencing social change. Why are some ideas replicated and virally shared, while others are discarded? There appears to be no formula. Although starting with an unamused cat will give you a fighting chance ... ■

Say hello to my little friend

IDEA № 54
THE DIGITAL WALLET

'Paper money is an ancient technology. You can run out of it. It wears out. It can get lost or stolen. In the twenty-first century, people need a form of money that's more convenient and secure, something that can be accessed from anywhere with an internet connection.'

With these words, Peter Thiel launched PayPal, an online payment system that changed the way the world does business. A year earlier, in December 1998, Thiel had co-founded Confinity, a remote payment platform for Palm Pilots. At the same time as Confinity launched its website, an online financial services company called X.com was launching its own site. Both companies were located on University Avenue in Palo Alto, California. In March 2000, the two companies merged. Confinity was too cold. X.com sounded like a porn site. The company name was changed to that of its most successful product – PayPal.

Two years later, eBay bought PayPal for $1.5 billion. It had beaten BillPoint, eBay's online payment system, at its own game. BillPoint was exclusive to eBay; PayPal could be used anywhere. And it offered $10 for every introduction. BillPoint was processing 4,000 transactions a day. PayPal was averaging 200,000. As eBay grew, so did PayPal. By April 2000, over a million eBay sellers were promoting PayPal. The masses had spoken.

Today, PayPal is available across 26 currencies, has over 100 million active accounts and processes almost $5,000 every second. As the digital wallet moves beyond the desktop to the smartphone, this dominance is under threat. Banks, credit-card companies, mobile-phone networks, Google, Amazon and radical new paradigms like Bitcoin are competing to be the payment platform of choice.

Whatever the future holds for PayPal, its legacy is immense and goes beyond reshaping global commerce. When venture capital dried up following the dot-com crash, the PayPal founders stepped in. They used money from the sale of PayPal to fund the second wave of Silicon Valley start-ups. eBay's money was used to finance Facebook, LinkedIn, Friendster, YouTube, Flickr, Digg, Last.fm, Spotify and many more Web 2.0 companies. Such is their influence that they collectively became known as the PayPal Mafia.

PayPal continues to work towards its ultimate ambition, to be a global currency in a cash-free future. If past performance is anything to go by, I wouldn't get in its way. ∎

'PayPal is available across 26 currencies, has over 100 million active accounts and processes almost $5,000 every second.'

The Paypal Mafia, so called because of the number of Web companies funded by the original PayPal team.

'After 20 years of putting shops on the Web, the Web is now appearing in shops.'

The Amazon Fulfilment Centre in Dunfermline, Scotland. At over 93,000m² (one million ft²), the warehouse is about the size of 14 football pitches.

Shop until your connection drops

ECOMMERCE

Pepperoni and mushroom with extra cheese. The first thing purchased on the Web was, you guessed it, a pizza. PizzaNet, Pizza Hut's website, allowed customers in Santa Cruz, California, to order online. It was the first ecommerce site.

In the early '90s many companies were reluctant to move into online retail. There was a big problem: security. It was relatively easy for hackers to intercept passwords, credit card numbers and other personal details. Netscape recognized that consumer confidence was non-negotiable. In 1995, it developed an encryption service called Secure Sockets Layer (SSL), making online shopping a much safer activity.

That year, an online book retailer opened its virtual doors. With the ability to stock millions of titles and a product that fitted through a letterbox, Amazon was an immediate success. Others saw the potential and the market flooded with ecommerce companies, selling everything from DVDs to pet food, regardless of profit. But the bubble burst. Only those with deep pockets survived. Amazon, now the world's largest online retailer, did not turn a profit until 2003, eight years after its launch.

Ecommerce is now booming. The US market is worth $200 billion and grows by 20 per cent every year. In some countries, a quarter of all purchases are made online. Never before has it been so easy to find products and compare prices. We can shop round the clock from the comfort of our homes. Retailers benefit too: no longer constrained by geographical limitations, they can reach more customers at less cost.

Ecommerce has brought us collaborative filtering, responsive design, banner ads, cookies, SSL and many more innovations we now take for granted. This is just the beginning. Deep personalization, offering individual pricing and unique deals, is just around the corner.

After 20 years of shops joining the Web, the Web is now creeping into shops. Interactive signage, **Quick Response codes**, image recognition and in-store pick-up are changing the face of retail.

It started with a pizza, and fast-food giant Pizza Hut remains at the cutting edge of electronic purchase. Its new application for the Xbox enables you to order a snack as you game: it seems every platform is after a slice of the ecommerce action. ∎

You might also like...

IDEA № 56
COLLABORATIVE FILTERING

Every day there are more webpages to visit, books to buy, music to listen to and films to watch. Search helps us to find stuff we know about – but what about the things we don't know about?

Collaborative filtering makes predictions about an individual's interests based on the interests of similar people. The underlying assumption is that if person A has the same opinion as person B on a particular issue, A is more likely to share B's opinion on a different issue than the opinion of a person chosen at random.

An early adopter of collaborative filtering was Alexa. In 1996, when a visitor arrived at a website, the Alexa toolbar provided a list of websites that had been visited by others who had viewed the same page. In 1999, Amazon acquired Alexa and adopted the technology, introducing its own form of collaborative filtering shortly afterwards.

For each book Amazon sells, it creates a 'neighbourhood' of related books based on other people's purchase history. Whenever you buy a book, Amazon recommends another book from that book's neighbourhood. This approach is shared by social book-marking services such as StumbleUpon and Digg. They identify users similar to you, i.e. users who have bookmarked similar pages to you, and suggest pages you might like to visit. Last.fm does the same for music. It builds a detailed profile of each user's musical taste based on the tracks that user listens to. Netflix does the same for films.

Collaborative filtering is now a fundamental part of our web experience. It helps people to find things they might otherwise miss, and helps online retailers to increase sales through cross-selling. Malcolm Gladwell describes collaborative filtering as 'a kind of doppelgänger search engine .... If you and your doppelgänger love the same ten books, chances are you'll also like the eleventh book he likes.'

As the Web matures, our willingness to divulge personal information is growing. In an increasingly connected world, this data is shared across sites and applications. The more personal data we provide and the more it is shared, the more recommendation engines will improve. Collaborative filters will develop tailored experiences based on our demographics and interests as well as our purchase history. Instead of our having to seek out information, collaborative filtering will bring it to us before we have even asked for it. I am sure other people like me would like that too. ■

If you like 100 Ideas that Changed the Web, *you might like these books too.*

Don't hold the front page

IDEA № 57

THE DRUDGE REPORT

When Matt Drudge was working in the gift shop at CBS in 1994, he started sending out studio gossip to a few friends via email. He called it the Drudge Report. A couple of years later, the newsletter moved to the Web, where it would change the face of journalism forever.

Matt Drudge, founder and editor of the Drudge Report.

During Bill Clinton's first term as president (1993–97), he was accused of sexual harassment by former state employee Paula Jones. Her lawyers subpoenaed women they suspected Clinton had had relationships with, one of these women was Monica Lewinsky. She denied it, which outraged her colleague Linda Tripp, who had taped conversations with Lewinsky admitting the affair. Tripp gave the tapes to Independent Counsel Kenneth Starr, who now had his smoking gun.

Reporter Michael Isikoff had been investigating the story for over a year and *Newsweek* was due to publish on Saturday 17 January 1998. Moments before the magazine was due to go to press, the editor pulled the story. Accusing the president of having sex with an intern in the Oval Office was just too big a deal: he needed time to double-check the facts. Matt Drudge got wind of the scandal that evening and had no such qualms. The story broke on the Drudge Report website shortly before midnight.

Web Posted: 01/17/98 23:32:47 PST -- NEWSWEEK KILLS STORY ON WHITE HOUSE INTERN BLOCKBUSTER REPORT: 23-YEAR OLD, FORMER WHITE HOUSE INTERN, SEX RELATIONSHIP WITH PRESIDENT
World Exclusive
Must Credit the DRUDGE REPORT
At the last minunte, at 6pm on Saturday evening, Newsweek magazine killed a story that was destined to shake official Washington to its foundation: a White House intern had carried on a sexual affair with the President of the United States!

Journalism would never be the same again. It was *Newsweek*'s story but the Drudge Report got the scoop; *Newsweek* had lost its nerve and paid the price. Clinton ignored the story until the *Washington Post* covered it three days

'*I did not have sexual relations with that woman.*' Bill Clinton, 26 January 1998.

later, when he famously claimed: 'I did not have sexual relations with that woman.'

Nine months later, the Starr Report was published on the Web. For the first time, if you were not online, you were missing history. This was 1998, the year before Blogger, six years before Facebook and eight years before Twitter. A lot of people were not online. That was soon to change. Web traffic doubled overnight – 20 million people read the report within 48 hours.

The Starr Report led to the second impeachment trial in history of a US president. Luckily for Clinton, the Senate decided that oral sex lay outside the definition of sexual relations as defined by the Court, and he was not convicted. Clinton survived the scandal but *Newsweek* never recovered. Fifteen years on, it does not exist, whereas the Drudge Report gets millions of visitors each month. (See also **Aggregation**.) ∎

'The dynamic feeds created at the turn of the century signified a maturing of the Web.'

Social aggregation services like Flipboard are the direct descendants of RSS.

A stepping stone to the real-time Web

IDEA № 58
RSS FEEDS

Really Simple Syndication (RSS) allows people to subscribe to timely updates from their favourite websites. More than this, it was a stepping stone to the real-time Web of today.

In 1997, Dave Winer, the man who gave us the blog, created the first RSS feed for his Scripting News website (see **Blogging**). Over the next couple of years, together with Dan Libby at Netscape, he refined and updated the format. Alternative syndication formats have also appeared, notably Atom in 2003, but it was Winer's format that gave us the widely accepted standard we use today.

According to Winer, 2002 was the tipping point. The *New York Times* began to offer its readers the option to subscribe to news articles via RSS, and many other news services and blogs followed suit. Such was the take-up that, in 2004, Mozilla Firefox incorporated RSS feeds into its browser. Microsoft followed in 2005, incorporating the now familiar orange icon in its Internet Explorer and Outlook products.

RSS feeds mean that content can be viewed as soon as it is published, without having to visit the individual websites. The news comes to you. This powerful functionality did not go unnoticed by the raft of social networks that emerged in the mid-2000s. The personalized news feeds produced by

'follows' and 'likes' display very similar functionality to RSS feeds, just in a more socially integrated way.

Traditional RSS feeds have now been usurped by social networks and visually rich, socially integrated readers such as Feedly, Feedspot and Flipboard. Google's decision to retire its popular Google Reader in favour of Google+ is telling; the way people consume content has fundamentally changed. RSS continues to be valued by those who prioritize speed and simplicity over social recommendations, but they are in the minority. Increasingly, we depend on our social circles for our news – the people we trust most are our friends.

Although RSS feeds are now in decline, the real-time Web they pioneered is on the ascent. The dynamic feeds created at the turn of the century signified a maturing of the Web. They bridged the gap between the static web of the '90s and the social web of the late 2000s, bringing about a lasting change in the way we consume online content. ■

Aged just 14, Aaron Swartz was a member of the working group that created the RSS 1.0 specification. He went on to help define RDF (Resource Description Framework) at the World Wide Web Consortium (W3C).

Hey you, get off my cloud

IDEA № 59

WEB STREAMING

On 24 June 1993, Severe Tire Damage performed the first live concert on the Net. Their 152 x 76-pixel live stream used about half the available bandwidth of the entire internet.

Severe Tire Damage (STD) were based in the San Francisco Bay area of California. Band members worked at Apple, DEC and Xerox PARC. In the summer of 1993, they were asked to play in Xerox PARC's car park, and they decided to stream the gig over the internet. Slightly worried about copyright, they rang Sony Music to check if they needed to pay royalties on a cover version they intended to perform. Sony's response was 'Music on the internet? Don't worry, it's not an issue.'

The following year, the Rolling Stones broadcast their *Voodoo Lounge* tour over the Net using the same technology, the Internet Multicast Backbone. Mick Jagger opened the concert saying, 'I want to say a special welcome to everyone that's climbed into the internet tonight and has got into the Mbone. I hope it doesn't all collapse.'

STD decided to open up for them – without asking. There was no way of locking down the channel – it was just open. STD's drummer compared it to the early days of flight. 'It was OK to land in a farmer's field because there weren't any other options. There's not many people using the internet in this way, so anything goes for now. We're still exploring brand new space.' The drummer was Mark Weiser, Chief Scientist at Xerox PARC, the father of ubiquitous computing.

The Stones play on, but the Mbone is no more. By the end of the 90s the technology had been replaced by RealNetworks, Windows Media Player and Quicktime. Web streaming was becoming mainstream. Seven years to the day after the first live gig, in June 2000, Bill Clinton's weekly radio address was broadcast on the Web.

A turning point came in 2002: Macromedia Flash 6.0 added video streaming. The Flash plug-in came pre-installed with many browsers, simplifying the process of watching online video. In 2005, ex-PayPal employees Chad Hurley, Steve Chen and Jawed Karim took the logical next step – they launched a video-sharing site.

YouTube is now the third most visited site on the Web. As with the internet's second ever live gig, amateur and professional content sits side by side (see **YouTube**). After STD gatecrashed the Rolling Stones' live streaming, Mick Jagger called them 'Furry Geeks', but he also went on to say the surprise opening act was 'a good reminder of the democratic nature of the internet.' Well said, Mick. ∎

Mick Jagger on the Rolling Stones Voodoo Lounge tour, which included the first mainstream concert to be broadcast on the internet.

'The Stones play on, but the Mbone is no more.'

'Cyberspace does not lie within your borders'

IDEA Nº 60

THE INDEPENDENCE OF CYBERSPACE

The Electronic Frontier Foundation is an international organization that campaigns to preserve personal freedoms on the internet.

In 1996, John Perry Barlow, lyricist for the Grateful Dead and co-founder of the Electronic Frontier Foundation, wrote a Declaration of the Independence of Cyperspace. It was a response to the US Government incorporating the internet within telecommunications law.

'Governments of the Industrial World, you weary giants of flesh and steel, I come from Cyberspace, the new home of Mind. On behalf of the future, I ask you of the past to leave us alone. You are not welcome among us. You have no sovereignty where we gather.'

Barlow's Declaration evokes the US Declaration of Independence, particularly the right to free speech. He described the internet as a borderless, stateless world where anyone, anywhere should be able to express his or her beliefs without fear of censorship. He called the 1996 Telecommunications Reform Act an insult to the dreams of the founding fathers of America, but he also directed his wrath at the governments of China and Europe.

Barlow went on to claim that information industries that treat speech and ideas as industrial products are obsolete. In the virtual world, thoughts can be reproduced and distributed infinitely at zero cost; the old rules of copyright no longer apply.

The Declaration has been widely criticized as the kind of utopian hippy dream you might expect from the lyricist of the Grateful Dead. Even Barlow himself later said, 'we all get older and smarter'. Yet it remains a good representation of many of the anti-censorship voices on the Web. The 2012 actions opposing the Stop Online Piracy Act (SOPA), the protests surrounding the US Government's treatment of hacktivist Aaron Swartz, and the **hacker** movement Anonymous, are all driven by a deeply held belief that the Web should not be censored.

However, a Web totally free of government intervention is both unrealistic and undesirable. Without government-funded research, neither the internet nor the Web would exist. Extreme views that incite hatred and violence have no place in society, virtual or otherwise. Criminal activity needs to be policed online as much as it does on the street.

What are needed are laws made for the era of the Web. Clumsily updated laws, made as a result of fear and paranoia, applied to a medium the lawmakers do not fully understand, are not a good solution for anyone. 'We will create a civilization of the Mind in Cyberspace. May it be more humane and fair than the world your governments have made before.' ∎

'Clumsily updated laws applied to a medium lawmakers do not understand are not a good solution.'

'*The Blair Witch Project* demonstrated that in the age of the Web, anyone could reach a global audience.'

1999's The Blair Witch Project changed how films were promoted. Artisan Entertainment had the vision to see the potential of the Web beyond an online trailer.

In October of 1994
three student filmmakers disappeared
in the woods near Burkittsville, Maryland
while shooting a documentary...

A year later their footage was found.

THE BLAIR WITCH PROJECT

'Oh, well done! I commend your pains,
And every one shall share i' th' gains'

IDEA № 61
THE BLAIR WITCH PROJECT

On 30 July 1999, a couple of amateur filmmakers released an indie flick that would challenge Hollywood's preconceptions about how to make and market a film.

The Blair Witch Project cost less than $50,000 to shoot. Filmmakers Eduardo Sánchez and Daniel Myrick developed a script around three students investigating a local legend. They provided the framework for the story and then dropped the cast on location with the camera equipment. Each day, the three actors would improvise the dialogue and shoot the film themselves. The hand-held, amateur-looking footage they shot gave the film a documentary feel.

The film was screened on 24 January 1999 at the Sundance Film Festival. The opening sequence portrayed the events as real. 'In October of 1994, three student filmmakers disappeared in the woods near Burkittsville, Maryland, while shooting a documentary .... A year later their footage was found.'

Artisan Entertainment picked up the film for $1 million, as intrigued by the background story as by the film itself. They created a website leveraging the idea that the film was the product of recovered videotapes. By adding police reports and interviews with grieving parents, they added to the mystery. Background information on the legend was supplied to online communities interested in the supernatural. Instead of broadcasting to the passive masses, interest was stoked in those most likely to talk about and share the legend.

As Sánchez puts it, 'We had created this whole mythology and I just kept massaging it and building more details into it. Really for us, it wasn't about creating this whole new way of marketing films. People are on the Web asking about this movie, how else are we going to get it to them?'

But create a new way to market films is exactly what they did. The weekend the film opened, Artisan bought a full-page ad in *Variety*. It read: 'Blairwitch.com ... 21,222,589 hits to date.' It was the first film advert promoting a website rather than the film itself. For the first time, the website was as much a destination as the film.

Shot by amateurs with virtually no filmmaking experience, *The Blair Witch Project* demonstrated that in the age of the Web, anyone could reach a global audience. And even more than that, if you engaged that audience, they would market the film for you. For free. The message of *The Blair Witch Project* resonated far beyond Burkittsville Woods. ∎

And justice for all?

IDEA Nº 62

PEER-TO-PEER

In 1999 Shawn Fanning created a downloadable program that allowed him to share music with his friends. He called it Napster. Within days the 19-year-old had a lot of friends – 1,500 of them. He had created the first peer-to-peer (P2P) network.

Downloaded, the story of Napster, was released in 2013.

A computer network that allowed the sharing of resources without the need for a central server was a radical departure from the model that had dominated the computer industry for 50 years. Shawn's uncle John Fanning invested in the fledgling company and Shawn's friend Sean Parker committed himself full time to the project. The three of them relocated to Silicon Valley, where they were treated like rock stars. Napster looked set to rewrite the rules for the digital era. Except the Recording Industry Association of America had other ideas and sued. The rules had not changed after all, at least not yet.

Metallica discovered that their entire back catalogue was on Napster and joined the fight. Drummer Lars Ulrich was sickened 'that our art is being traded like a commodity rather than the art that it is.' In truth, whether it was art was not the issue – it was all about getting paid for the commodity. Dr. Dre followed suit, piling on the pressure by suing 300,000 fans who had illegally downloaded his music. It was too much for Napster. Despite support from some bands such as Public Enemy and Radiohead, it shut down in July 2001 and declared itself bankrupt in 2002.

It was the end of Napster but it was not the end of P2P. Open-source developers set about creating a second generation of P2P software products without the central indexing function that had been Napster's downfall. Mainstream players also took note, AOL, Yahoo and Microsoft all adding file-swapping ability to their instant-messaging products. Eventually, a dominant P2P protocol emerged. It was called BitTorrent, and with 150 million active users it is now responsible for 10 per cent of all internet traffic – more than Facebook and YouTube combined.

'Our art is being traded like a commodity rather than the art it is.'

Lars Ulrich of Metallica confronts Hank Barry, CEO of Napster, while Roger McGuinn (seated left) of The Byrds looks on.

Napster provided a radical new model for file distribution, the impact of which has spread far beyond the music industry: using the same decentralized model, Airbnb has become an accepted part of the short-term property rental market, and Buzzcar looks to do the same for vehicle hire. Perhaps the most surprising sector to be shaken up by the P2P model is the financial industry. Bitcoins, a peer-to-peer currency, are exchanged without an intermediate financial institution, and P2P lenders such as Zopa provide loans to small business, offering decent returns to investors by distributing the risk across many lenders.

Shawn Fanning went on to develop Rupture, a social network for gamers, and Path, a social network that limits connections to 150. Sean Parker was the first investor in Facebook and is now a board member of Spotify, a legitimate music-streaming platform based on the P2P software model. Not bad for a couple of college drop-outs. In the end, it seems the rules have changed, and even Lars Ulrich recognizes it. At a recent press event, he shook hands with Sean Parker and agreed to put Metallica's back catalogue on Spotify. ∎

The need for speed

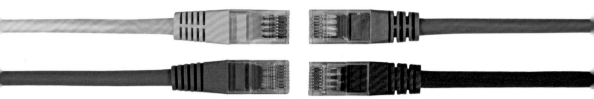

IDEA Nº63
BROADBAND

In 1999, only one in five UK homes were online. By 2009, the figure was four out of five. That is not surprising. Before broadband the Web did not really work.

It turns out the one thing we dislike more than a slow internet connection is paying for a faster one.

Since the telegraph, copper wires have been used to help us to communicate over long distances. Copper is highly conductive, strong and pliable. Copper wires formed the basis of the first telephone networks and still dominate telecommunications infrastructure to this day.

Digging up the entire telephone network and replacing it with fibre optics is expensive. Consequently, a lot of thought has gone into how to squeeze every last kilobyte of speed out of the existing system.

In the late 90s, Integrated Services Digital Network (ISDN) emerged as a faster alternative to dial-up connections. Data carried over ISDN is transmitted at a higher frequency than voice data, so it could support the internet and the telephone at the same time. This was a big step forward, but the relatively high cost of the 128k service limited its popularity to businesses.

Broadband appeared at the turn of the century. Digital subscriber lines (DSL) convert existing copper telephone wire into a data link 30 times the speed of a 56k modem. Replacing a single band with separate bands for uploading, downloading and voice speeds things up. Instead of a single, narrow band you get a broader band. Allocate more bandwidth to downstream traffic than upstream and connection speeds are further enhanced. Almost 15 years later, asymmetric digital subscriber line (ADSL) is still the most common form of broadband.

Broadband meant the Web could finally compete with TV on its own terms. YouTube began broadcasting in 2005; without broadband, no one would have been watching. Without broadband, graphically rich network games, video conferencing, the streaming of music and many dynamic web services we now take for granted would not be possible.

As the technological curve accelerates, so does our need for faster internet connectivity. From megabytes to gigabytes and now terabytes, our capacity to create ever-larger digital assets means that we need even greater bandwidth to manage them. Moore's Law (after Intel co-founder Gordon Moore) suggests that computing power doubles every 18 months; unfortunately Nielsen's Law (after Jakob Nielsen, see **User-centred Design**) predicts that connection speeds double every two years.

When the Web launched, standard dial-up modem speeds were 14k. A slow broadband connection today is 4Mb. That is 300 times faster, yet still we complain. If Jakob Nielsen is right, we always will. ■

Copyleft

CREATIVE COMMONS

Folk hero Woody Guthrie wrote in the 1940s: 'This song is copyrighted in US for a period of 28 years, and anybody caught singin' it without our permission, will be mighty good friends of ourn, cause we don't give a dern. Publish it. Write it. Sing it. Swing to it. Yodel it. We wrote it, that's all we wanted to do.'

While not all rights owners are quite as generous, there are varying degrees to which people wish to protect their work. Intellectual property laws are usually black and white – you either retain or relinquish copyright. Motivated by the introduction of the 1998 Sonny Bono Copyright Term Extension Act, Eric Eldred, Lawrence Lessig and Hal Abelson decided that there must be a middle way.

Eldred, Lessig and Abelson formed the Creative Commons (CC) organization, with the aim of creating copyright licenses that embrace the collaborative spirit of the Web. Creative Commons builds on the work of Richard Stallman's Free Software Foundation, founded in 1983 (see **Open Source**). It applies similar principles to work beyond software and offers a variety of licences. With these licences, rights are retained but additional permissions are granted to allow others to share, adapt and, in certain circumstances, even sell the work. The six different licences give creators more choice in how freely others might use their work.

Despite protests from intellectual rights campaigners, who claim that its licences cloud copyright issues,

Creative Commons clarifies the situation for many. The 'copyleft' licences, and their associated icons, are easy to understand and implement. They replace the individual negotiations necessary under an 'all rights reserved' system with a 'some rights reserved' arrangement.

This new way of sharing and distributing work had a huge kick start when it was adopted by the photo-sharing site Flickr. Wikipedia followed, and there are now approaching a billion CC licences in use. Creative Commons also has the backing of influential – and perhaps surprising – supporters, such as Microsoft and Google. Microsoft Office has an add-in that allows users to embed Creative Commons licences directly into Word, PowerPoint and Excel documents, while Google incorporates a search for CC-licensed documents and images.

There is a way to go, but perhaps it is only a matter of time before everyone thinks Creative Commons first, copyright second. ∎

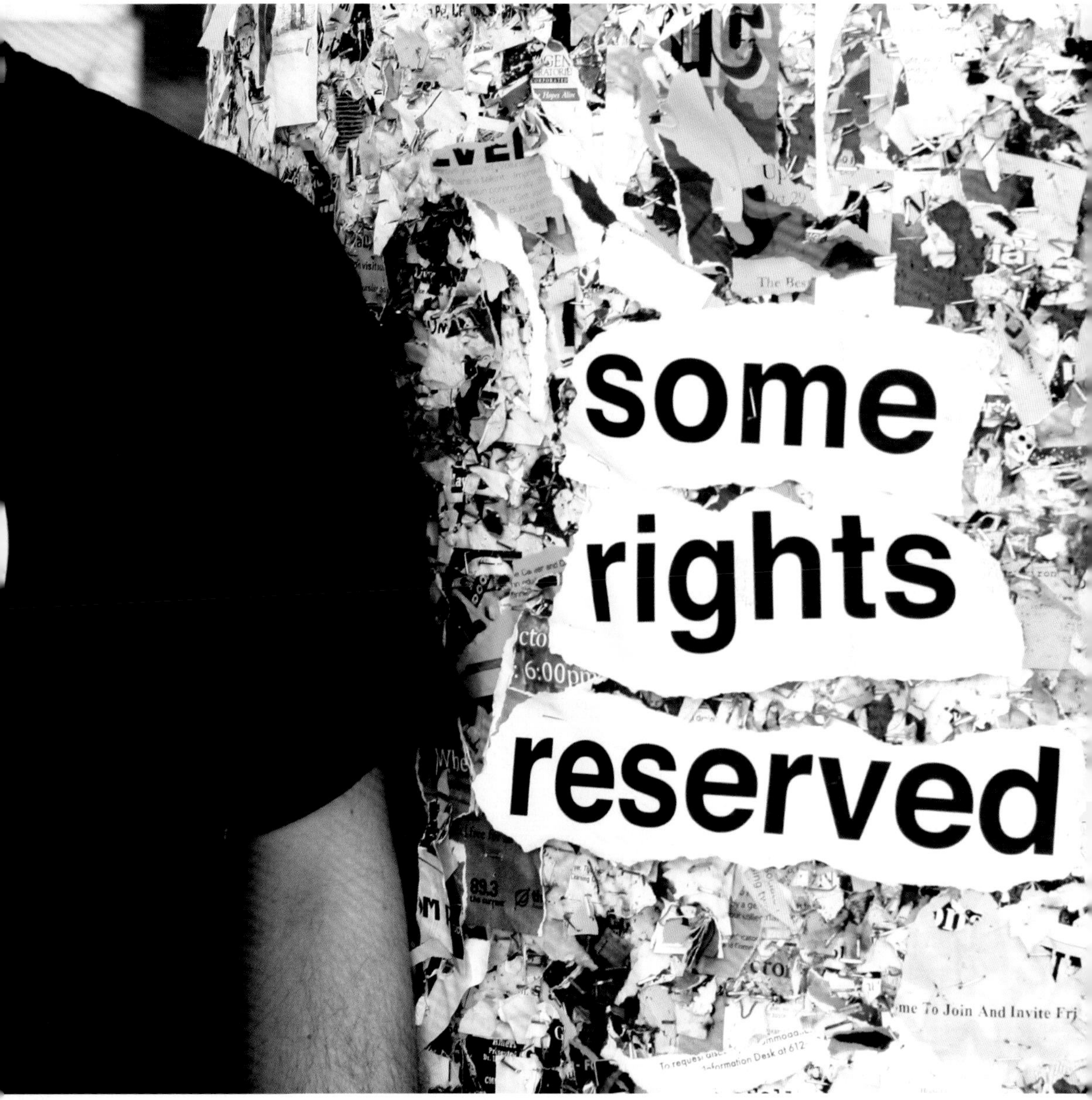
some
rights
reserved

'Low interest rates, easily available venture capital and rapidly rising share prices meant traditional measures of company performance were ignored.'

The dot-com bubble reached its climax on 10 March 2000. Over the next 18 months $5 trillion was wiped off the value of US companies. Many dot-coms ran out of capital and were liquidated.

Get large or get lost

IDEA № 65
THE DOT-COM BUBBLE

In 1637 the price of a single tulip bulb was ten times the average annual income. Many investors were ruined by the drastic fall in prices that followed. 'Tulip mania' was the first recorded speculative bubble.

When investors buy shares because of rapidly rising prices, rather than because the shares are undervalued, a bubble occurs. Sooner or later that bubble bursts.

This is exactly what happened during the dot-com bubble of the late 90s. Low interest rates, easily available venture capital and rapidly rising share prices meant traditional measures of company performance were ignored. The accepted dot-com model was to expand a customer base as rapidly as possible, even if it produced large losses. Profit would come later. 'Get large or get lost' was the wisdom of the day. Such was the hysteria that, if a company added .com to the end of its name, its share price shot through the roof overnight. Over a three-year period, from 1997 to 2000, the share value of web-based businesses rose rapidly, before dramatically crashing in March 2000.

When the market fell, loss-making dot-com businesses could no longer depend on investment to keep afloat. One of the first to collapse was the fashion retailer boo.com. It had spent almost $200 million in less than a year. Lavish spending aside, the company failed because its technology was too sophisticated for the market. Too few people were online and too few of them had connection speeds fast enough to use the site as it was intended. This was typical. Dot-com companies, often run by inexperienced but computer-savvy entrepreneurs, were technology-driven rather than market-driven. Many companies failed, others limped on. Those that had financial reserves, like Amazon and eBay, held fast and recovered to become the web-retailing giants of today (see **The Long Tail**).

Despite the vast sums of money lost, it was not all wasted. Traditional businesses were forced to transform, huge amounts were invested in infrastructure, exciting new companies emerged, and people grew used to interacting and transacting online. The bubble accelerated the advancement of the Web and, in doing so, changed our world completely. Many of the dot-com companies that crashed had sound ideas but poor business models; they over-invested in an immature medium. Fifteen years later, the dot-com vision has become reality. Selling pet food online was never a bad idea. Investing $300 million to do so always was. ∎

'Regular viewers felt betrayed, but many more tuned in.'

Lonelygirl15 focused on the life of a teenage girl named Bree. The YouTube video blog was eventually proved as a hoax, Bree being played by 19-year-old actress Jessica Lee Rose.

Interactive television or a passive Web?

IDEA № 66

WEB TV

In 1997, in their article, 'PUSH! Kiss your browser goodbye: The radical future of media beyond the Web', Kevin Kelly and Gary Wolf suggest that web TV is the stage before true interaction takes place.

'All new media recapitulate the evolution of former media, until the new media eventually achieve their own limits. So online media have evolved from smoke signals (email) to books and magazines (the Web). We are now about to arrive at television (push media), before we finally emerge into what interactivity is really about.'

Web TV made its first tentative steps in 1995. Advertising agency Fattal & Collins released *The Spot*, the first soap opera on the Web, sponsored by Intel, Visa and Apple. The characters kept online diaries and posted photos and video on the site, and visitors could email the cast, their advice becoming part of the storyline. At its peak, the site was receiving 100,000 visits a day.

The release of Macromedia Flash in 1996 brought animation to the Web. Almost immediately, *The Goddamn George Liquor Program*, created by John Kricfalusi of *Ren & Stimpy* fame, demonstrated that the Web could compete with TV on its own terms. Co-founder of the animation company Spümcø, John K was notorious for falling out with TV networks, infamously being fired by CBS for depicting Mighty Mouse snorting white powder. He repeated this trick at Nickelodeon. In slow-motion, graphic detail, Ren bludgeoned his owner, George Liquor, into a vegetative state with an oar. John K was fired again.

Determined to make undiluted cartoons, Spümcø's next project bypassed TV networks entirely. Launching online, where Kricfalusi. could create cartoons free from censorship, the first cartoon series made for the Web launched in October 1997. Featuring talking dog turds, extreme violence and sexual innuendo, *The Goddamn George Liquor Program* pushed the boundaries of taste way beyond TV norms. As John K. said at the time, 'You can do it any way you want on the Net.'

The launch of YouTube in 2005 stimulated a flurry of 'webisodes', the most popular being 2006's 'Lonelygirl15', the video blog of teenager Bree Avery. Millions of people were enthralled by her everyday life, but suspicions were raised when her parents were kidnapped by a cult. Soon after, it was revealed that 16-year-old Bree was actually 19-year-old actress Jessica Lee Rose. Regular viewers felt betrayed, but many more tuned in.

Award-winning shows like *House of Cards* have demonstrated that TV has moved beyond traditional networks, but hopes that the Web would make TV less passive are yet to be realized. It turns out that the Web does not replace all other media, but integrates them into a single place. At the moment, Web TV just means more TV. ∎

'All Wiki content is work in progress.'

On 25 March 1995, Ward Cunningham launched WikiWikiWeb, named after the Wiki Wiki Shuttle at Honolulu International Airport.

'Be good and play nice!'

THE WIKI

Documents that can be edited simultaneously by multiple people are now commonplace. Before Ward Cunningham invented the wiki in 1995, this was not so easy.

Ward Cunningham, inventor of the wiki.

In the early '90s, the state-of-the-art collaboration tool was the LISTSERV. When an email is sent to a LISTSERV mailing list, it is automatically broadcast to everyone on the list. Ward Cunningham noticed that older messages were lost, buried under the more recent posts. He proposed that messages were collated on webpages, which would be collectively edited. As he explained, 'Think of it as a moderated list where anyone can be moderator and everything is archived. It's not quite a chat, still, conversation is possible.' On 25 March 1995, Cunningham launched WikiWikiWeb, named after the Wiki Wiki Shuttle at Honolulu International Airport. Originally, he was going to call it QuickWeb, but he changed his mind when he learned *wiki* was the Hawaiian word for 'hurry'. The name is apt. From WikiWikiWeb: 'All Wiki content is work in progress. Most of all, this is a forum where people share ideas! It changes as people come and go.'

Cunningham gave away the source code and wikis became common in the programming community. However, it was not until the launch of Wikipedia in 2001 that the wiki became mainstream. Now the sixth most popular website in the world, Wikipedia has more than 3 million articles, all written, edited and maintained by the crowd.

There are now wikis for subjects ranging from *Star Wars* (Wookieepedia) to classified government information (WikiLeaks). Despite criticism of the reliability of the information, they function very well. In December 2005, the journal *Nature* compared the accuracy of articles from Wikipedia and *Encyclopaedia Britannica*. Across 42 articles, four serious errors were found in Wikipedia and four in *Encyclopaedia Britannica*, although Wikipedia's articles were often 'poorly structured'.

Wikis perhaps owe their success to the guiding principles put forward by Ward Cunningham back in 1995. He encouraged people to write only factual information, to avoid abstract advice and to be concise. His most important advice was perhaps contained in the way he signed off – 'Above all, be good and play nice!' ■

A picture paints
a thousand words

IDEA № 68
INFOGRAPHICS

Infographics present complex data in an easily digestible way. Exploiting the brain's innate ability to process visual information, they help us to comprehend complex data quickly and accurately.

The Web has given us access to more information than ever before. This volume of data demands new ways of navigating it. David McCandless, author of *Information is Beautiful*, says that 'by visualizing information, we turn it into a landscape that you can explore with your eyes, a sort of information map. When you're lost in information, an information map is kind of useful.'

Providing information visually is not new. Human beings have been using marks, painting images and drawing maps for thousands of years. However, true information graphics are less than 100 years old. It was in 1925, at the Social and Economic Museum of Vienna, that Otto Neurath invented information graphics as we recognize them today.

Neurath's vision was to bring 'dead statistics' to life by making them visually attractive. His maxim was: 'To remember simplified pictures is better than to forget accurate figures.' Originally called the Vienna Method, and later ISOTYPE (International System Of TYpographic Picture Education), the graphic language he pioneered is now ubiquitous, appearing everywhere, from airports to websites.

While Neurath gave us the pictogram, the statistician Edward Tufte is the pioneer of data visualization. His Data Density principle suggests that the more data is depicted, the better. In order to simplify a chart, reduce its scale rather than reduce the data. Counterintuitively, shrinking most graphs improves legibility. The Data-Ink Ratio recommends that the ink used to represent data should be greater than the ink used to show non-data. 'Chartjunk', the unnecessary use of graphical effects, should be omitted entirely. The Lie Factor assesses the graphical integrity of the chart; the size of effect shown in the graphic should reflect the size of effect shown in the data.

The rise of the social web and our reluctance to read long documents has propelled the work of information designers like Neurath, Tufte and McCandless to the fore. It is boom time for infographics. Alongside other bite-sized, shareable content such as photos of kittens and GIF animations, infographics have become a staple part of our media diet.

Occurring at the intersection of art and science, infographics appeal to both creative and analytical thinkers. Done badly, you get Chartjunk. Done well, they make data meaningful and entertaining. Sometimes even beautiful. ■

An infographic from Information is Beautiful *by David McCandless.*

What is Consciousness?
Make Up Your Own Mind

A field that exists in its own parallel 'realm' of existence outside reality so can't be seen.
(*Substance Dualism*)

A sensation that 'grows' inevitably out of complicated brain states.
(*Emergent Dualism*)

A physical property of all matter, like electromagnetism, just not one the scientists know about.
(*Property Dualism*)

All matter has a psychic part. Consciousness is just the psychic part of our brain.
(*Pan Psychism*)

Simply, mental states are physical events that we can see in brain scans.
(*Identity Theory*)

Consciousness and its states (belief, desire, pain) are simply functions the brain performs.
(*Functionalism*)

Literally just behavior. When we behave in a certain way, we appear conscious.
(*Behaviourism*)

An accidental side-effect of complex physical processes in the brain.
(*Epiphenomenalism*)

Not sure. But quantum physics, over classical physics, can better explain it.
(*Quantum Consciousness*)

The sensation of your most significant thoughts being highlighted.
(*Cognitivism*)

Consciousness is just higher order thoughts (thoughts about other thoughts).
(*Higher Order Theory*)

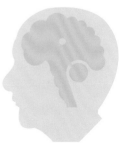

A continuous stream of ever-recurring phenomena, pinched, like eddies, into isolated minds.
(*Buddhism*)

Reality is broken, so
let's try something else

IDEA Nº 69

AUGMENTED REALITY

In 1955, Morton Heilig detailed his vision of a cinematic experience that engaged all the senses. Then in 1962, he built the Sensorama, a mechanical device that combined stereoscopic 3D images, stereo sound, smells and movement.

The first virtual reality (VR) machine was quickly followed by others. In 1966, the US Air Force created the first flight simulator, and in 1968, Ivan Sutherland created the first head-mounted VR system. It was so heavy it had to be suspended from the ceiling, and gained the nickname the Sword of Damocles. In 1978, the Aspen Movie Map was made at MIT – a virtual simulation of the town of Aspen, it was an early version of Google Street View (see **Surrogate Travel**).

Until recently, successful applications of VR were restricted to training simulations and gaming. In the mid-80s, Jaron Lanier founded VPL Research, the first company to sell virtual reality goggles, and Nintendo released the Power Glove, but adoption was poor.

It was not until the emergence of the iPhone that VR became mainstream. Apps such as Blippar use the phone's camera to enhance rather than replace real-world environments. In a process known as augmented reality, the camera or webcam is used to identify an object and then overlay it with computer-generated graphics. Global Positioning Systems (GPS), accelerometers and solid-state compasses enhance the in-built environment further.

Examples of augmented reality are plentiful, from commercial applications, such as estate agents showing which houses on a street are for sale, to

educational apps that annotate the night sky. When seen for the first time, the results are truly magical.

The latest developments in VR, like Oculus Rift, have come full circle, back to the headsets first envisioned in the 1960s. However, rather than a helmet suspended from the ceiling, technologies such as Google Glass are embedded in a neat pair of spectacles. In the future,

The Blippar app uses image recognition technology to add interactive advertising to real-world objects.

NASA's Virtual Interface Environment Workstation (VIEW), created in 1985, consisted of a wide-angle stereoscopic display unit, speech recognition and gesture-tracking devices.

displays will be integrated into people's normal eyewear.

Criticism of permanently layering the Web over our daily lives has been widespread, ranging from the potential to insert advertising, to privacy and safety concerns. It is interesting to note that these are the same concerns that greeted radio 100 years ago. ∎

'In future, displays will be integrated into actual eyewear.'

Can machines think?

CAPTCHA

A distorted chain of words known as a CAPTCHA.

In the dystopian sci-fi film *Blade Runner* (1982), the Voight-Kampff test employs more than 100 questions to determine if Rachael is a 'replicant'. The reality is much simpler.

The interrogation performed by Harrison Ford's Rick Deckard is a form of Turing Test, a concept introduced by Alan Turing in his 1950 paper 'Computing Machinery and Intelligence'. The paper opens with the words, 'I propose to consider the question, can machines think?', and goes on to describe how this might be proved. At the heart of this test is a machine's ability to exhibit intelligent behaviour indistinguishable from that of a human.

Fifty years after Turing's paper, the Web was booming but there was one huge problem – spam. Automated scripts were bombarding websites with links to sites selling fake designer goods and illicit pharmaceutical products. Twenty-two-year-old Luis von Ahn turned his thoughts towards the Turing Test. Originally, he thought of showing a web user an easily recognizable image, like an elephant, and asking them to identify it. It turns out we are not very good at recognizing elephants. His next idea was to get users to identify a distorted sequence of letters. It worked. He called his invention a CAPTCHA, for Completely Automated Public Turing test to tell Computers and Humans Apart.

In fact, CAPTCHA is a Reverse Turing Test. A computer, rather than a human, spots the difference. The point at which software can consistently pass the Reverse Turing Test is not too far away. In the meantime, von Ahn has figured out a clever way to make positive use of CAPTCHA. Sometimes a CAPTCHA has two strings of distorted letters rather than one. The second is called a RECAPTCHA. Von Ahn has partnered with the Internet Archive, a not-for-profit organization that scans books and puts them online. When its scanners find a word they cannot read, it is turned into a RECAPTCHA. When enough humans decipher it consistently, the result is added to the text. Every day, about 200 million CAPTCHAs are deciphered and millions of words are digitized. It is nice to know that humans are still good for something. ∎

Luis von Ahn, inventor of the CAPTCHA.

Nude girls and kittens

IDEA № 71
PHOTO SHARING

Before the Large Hadron Collider, LHC stood for Les Horribles Cernettes, a doo-wop band made up of CERN employees. In 1992, a photo of the group was the first image uploaded to the Web.

The photographer was Silvano de Gennaro, a developer at CERN, who managed the band. His co-worker Tim Berners-Lee was looking for an image to test a new version of his browser that could support images. So a badly Photoshopped image was the first picture on the Web. It was a sign of things to come.

Surprisingly, brands like Kodak were slow to take advantage of this new opportunity. Despite developing a digital camera in 1975, Kodak stuck stubbornly to film, fearful of sabotaging its own business model. It was burying its head in the sand. The mass adoption of digital cameras in the late '90s brought with it a number of sites where you could upload and store images. The first – Webshots – was launched in 1999. Others such as Photobucket, Picasa and Yahoo! Photos followed in the early 2000s.

As digital cameras became cheaper, photo-sharing came into its own. Launching in 2004, a year before Facebook and YouTube, Flickr soon became the premier image-hosting site. Allowing you to share your pictures, and follow and connect with other users, it was much more than a photo-sharing platform. It was a social network.

Slow to react to the smartphone revolution, Flickr left space for the competition. Originally starting out as a geolocation service, Instagram saw that Foursquare had beaten them to it. It changed its focus to one simple aspect of its service – photos. Allowing users to share photos on the move gave it the edge. Also offering simple filters to make images look better (and the photographers' lives look cooler), Instagram usurped Flickr as the photo-sharing platform of choice.

Recently, sites like Pinterest have added a new twist to photo sharing, allowing users to repost or pin images from across the Web to create themed moodboards. Now everybody can be a curator.

The Web has become an extension of our identities. Displaying our interests, or at least the interests we wish to present to the world, offers friends and followers a snapshot of our personality. There is no easier way to do this than through images. We are what we share. Must be a lot of nude girls and kittens surfing the Web. ∎

Penelope Umbrico's Sunset Portraits from 11,827,282 Flickr Sunsets on 01/07/13 *highlights the futility of individual assertion through a cultural meme. The title of the artwork reflects the ever-growing number of sunset pictures on Flickr. As this number only lasts an instant, its recording is analogous to the act of photographing the sunset itself.*

'Launching in 2004, Flickr was much more than a photo-sharing platform. It was a social network.'

The download festival

PODCAST

A podcast is a digital file, originally made for downloading to a portable media player. While today's versions are just as likely to be video files, the earliest examples were audio only.

The name podcast was coined by journalist Ben Hammersley in 2004. Before they had a name, audio blogs like Germany's Tonspion (1998) and Buzzgrinder (2001) in the US published songs shared by artists and record labels. Downloaded to an MP3 player, these digital mix tapes proved a great means of promoting new acts. The format was popularized by blog and RSS pioneer Dave Winer in 2000. His software package Radio UserLand introduced additional functionality to **RSS feeds**. With it, listeners could subscribe to their favourite audio blogs and automatically download files as they were posted.

The launch of the iPod in 2001 accelerated the adoption of digital music. It also provided a platform for downloading shows like the *Daily Source Code*, hosted by ex-MTV DJ Adam Curry, and CBC's technology show, */Nerd*.

Downloading a podcast became even simpler in 2005, when iTunes included in-built support for podcasts. While it was easier for the listener, it had a stunting effect on the industry. Podcasts needed to be compatible with iTunes if they wanted a sizeable audience. On top of this, while Apple accepted that 'podcast' had become a generic term, it threatened legal action against any service with 'pod' in its name.

In 2005, the launch of the fifth-generation iPod, which supported video, meant podcasts went multimedia. Home-made TV shows, amateur films and video blogs all became popular. Broadcast media couldn't ignore the phenomenon any longer. Established TV channels, radio stations and newspapers adopted the format. TV channels offered previews, reviews and selective downloads. Radio stations compiled weekly highlight podcasts of their more popular shows.

The podcast added another dimension to self-publishing but, more significantly, it redefined how we watch TV and listen to the radio. No longer tied to a traditional media schedule, we now consume our favourite shows where we want, whenever we want. ∎

'No longer tied to a traditional media schedule, we now consume our favourite shows where we want, whenever we want.'

A pedestrian passes a wall covered with iPod adverts in July 2005. Apple had just reported its best quarterly profit ever, largely thanks to the iPod.

'An embarrassment of niches'

HEAD

Popularity

IDEA № 73

THE LONG TAIL

The long tail is what happens when everything is available to everyone. Given enough choice and enough customers, obscure products tailored to our individual needs are more desirable than mass-market blockbusters.

In statistics, the long tail refers to distributions with a large number of occurrences far from the head of the spread. They arise when a large proportion of data points are unusually far from the mean.

The term has gained popularity in recent times as a description of the online retailing strategy of selling small quantities of lots of unique items.

The concept was popularized by Chris Anderson in his 2006 book *The Long Tail: Why the Future of Business Is Selling Less of More*. Anderson suggests that the future of business does not lie in the high-volume end of a traditional demand curve – the blockbusters – but in what used to be regarded as misses, the long, thin, straggly end of the demand curve. Now that consumers can find products tailored to their interests, they will bypass those

products designed for mass appeal. Anderson takes this further, suggesting that the tail will grow steadily longer and fatter, as consumers discover more products better suited to their tastes. Technology writer Kevin Kelleher describes this as 'an embarrassment of niches'. The global reach of the Web means that a large number of disparate, niche audiences can be combined to make one large, economically valuable market. A significant portion of Amazon's sales, for example, come from obscure books that are not available in high-street stores.

For digital products like music and e-books, storage and distribution costs approach zero. The viable tail of the demand curve is therefore extremely long. Apple's iTunes lists millions of songs, whereas the largest high-street record stores can only hope to stock thousands.

'We sold more books today that didn't sell at all yesterday than we sold today of all the books that did sell yesterday.'

Chris Anderson, author of the 2006 book The Long Tail: Why the Future of Business Is Selling Less of More.

Throw search into the mix, so that people can find these obscure products, and you have the perfect conditions for the long tail to succeed.

The Web has transformed our world. The immediate gratification and near-infinite choices it offers have overturned traditional business models and revealed new truths about how consumers like to shop.

Amazon's Josh Petersen sums it up: 'We sold more books today that didn't sell at all yesterday than we sold today of all the books that did sell yesterday.' You might need to read that a couple of times. ∎

LONG TAIL

'A seamless combination of software and data.'

WasteLandscape, *by Elise Morin, is a 500m² (5,382ft²) artificial undulating landscape of 65,000 unsold CDs.*

A Web that works

AJAX

Short for 'asynchronous JavaScript and XML', AJAX is a group of interrelated web-programming technologies that can send and retrieve data in the background, without having to reload the page.

In the early years of the Web, pages were built entirely in HTML. On each click, a new page was loaded. Even a small change to the page meant the entire page had to be refreshed. On the plus side, it was easy to create webpages; on the down side, it led to a stop-start user experience.

In 1999, Internet Explorer 5 introduced the XMLHttpRequest, using it to dynamically update the news stories on the MSN homepage. This functionality was soon adopted by all major browsers, and the Web made a gradual transition from static to dynamic pages. The roots of AJAX had been established.

Then, in 2004, John Battelle and Tim O'Reilly held the first Web 2.0 Conference. Their opening remarks, described the future of the Web as a platform. Whereas Web 1.0 companies, such as Netscape, created software for the Web, Web 2.0 companies, like Google, created software on the Web.

Over the next couple of years Google confirmed Battelle and O'Reilly's prediction. Services such as Gmail, Google Maps and Google Calendar were more like software than webpages. In February 2005, Jesse James Garrett assessed the technologies these services were built on and described them collectively as AJAX. The term stuck.

Web 2.0 companies that base their services on AJAX share few of the characteristics of a traditional software company. Their software does not come in a box. There is no licence and no scheduled releases, just ongoing improvement.

AJAX represents a fundamental shift in what is possible on the Web. Not only does it eliminate the stop-start nature of websites, but it also reduces the amount of data transferred between the server and the browser, and so speeds up response times. Websites become a seamless combination of software and data. In fact, the data is central to Web 2.0 companies: Google has an index of links, Google Maps has geographical data, Amazon a catalogue of products, Flickr an image collection, Facebook a dossier of our lives.

AJAX technologies allow web applications to access these databases in a fluid and meaningful way. They move websites beyond pages to dynamic environments that are a joy to explore. Web 2.0 is not hyperbole, it's a useful description of a Web that works. ∎

'Social networks are the defining technology of our time.'

A portrait of Facebook founder, Mark Zuckerberg, composed of original Facebook icons. Made by Charis Tsevis, based on a photo by Marcio Jose Sanchez, for WIRED magazine.

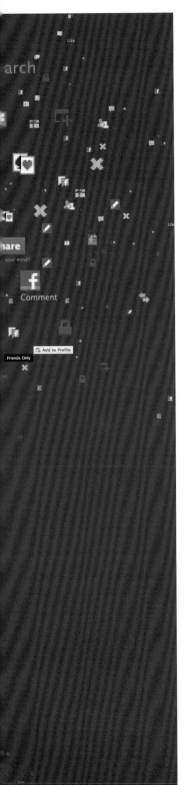

What's on your mind?

SOCIAL NETWORKING

With a billion active users, Facebook is the largest human network the world has ever known. It is The Social Network.

Thefacebook.com launched in February 2004, an online version of Harvard's student directory. Mark Zuckerberg said at the time, 'Everyone's been talking a lot about a universal face book within Harvard. I think it's kind of silly that it would take the University a couple of years to get around to it as I can do it better than they can, and I can do it in a week.' Within 24 hours there were over 1,000 sign-ups. Within the first month, more than half the students at Harvard had registered.

In 2005, Facebook became available to every college student in the US. In September 2006, it was open to everyone in the world aged thirteen or older. Now with more than a billion users, it is the second most popular site on the web and is gaining on Google fast.

Social networks satisfy our need to connect with one another. They feed our interest in one another's lives. The social life we once found in our communities, we now find online. Only we don't catch up over the garden fence. A steady flow of news and views is delivered directly to our computer screen, from all over the world. The removal of geographical boundaries exposes us to a wider range of views and cultures. By opening up our social circles beyond our local community, social networks open up our minds.

Whether we're sharing world events or gossip, our lives are being documented as never before. Zuckerberg believes a more transparent world makes us better citizens. It also happens to be very lucrative. Facebook collects more personal data than any other organization on earth. Every time we connect with a friend, post a comment or hit the like button, we volunteer valuable information. Facebook knows more about us than we know about ourselves. And it sells this information to the highest bidder. We accept it because we can no longer opt out. Like the telephone and the television, it has become an intrinsic part of our lives.

Social networks are the defining technology of our time. In less than a decade, they have become our primary source of news and an indispensable communication tool. The cost is our privacy. ∎

Tags, tag cloud, social tagging,
collaborative tagging, social classification

IDEA № 76
FOLKSONOMIES

One of the defining aspects of Web 2.0 is that users can tailor their online experience. A core part of this involves tagging. Nobody tells you what tags to use. You can make them up. And the more people who tag, the more relevant the tagging becomes. This is folksonomy.

The term 'folksonomy', taxonomy by folk, was coined in 2004 by Thomas Vander Wal. It describes the act of tagging web content, such as pictures, articles, music and webpages. Unlike folksonomy's etymological parent, taxonomy, tags can be assigned without any fixed hierarchy. The most pertinent terms naturally rise to the top, creating a more intuitive online experience.

Vander Wal identifies two types of folksonomy: broad and narrow. A narrow folksonomy occurs when there are only a few people tagging an object. A broad folksonomy is constructed by many different users. Some tags are used frequently, but the majority are peripheral. At the head of the distribution, they tend towards a consensus. If one person applies the tag 'Net Art' to an object, it does not have much value; if many people use this tag, then it is likely that the content is related to Net Art. That is not to say the long tail of less frequently used tags has no value. Obscure tags allow niche audiences to find content that they might not otherwise discover.

A platform that employs a narrow folksonomy is Flickr. With more than 50 million members and over 6 billion images, the need for search filters is obvious. A tagging system distributes the task over the entire population of Flickr users, and so the vast number of images become useful data at little or no cost. The reason it is a narrow folksonomy is because only the person who uploads a photograph can tag it. Conversely, Pinterest employs a broad folksonomy – anybody can tag any image.

In the tradition of the Web, folksonomies are hugely democratic. The power is in the hands of the users. The benefits of this anarchic, crowdsourced system of classification are perhaps surprising. Not only are folksonomies highly efficient, more comprehensive and more accurate than traditional methods, but their great strength is that the vocabulary of users is built in. ∎

A tag cloud of the authors of
the 100 best books, as proposed
by 100 writers from 54 different
countries, compiled and organized in
2002 by the Norwegian Book Club.

Release early and release often

PERPETUAL BETA

Traditionally, when software is released it has been through a comprehensive testing process. Features (and bugs) are baked in. Perpetual beta turns this on its head. Continuous improvement and constant updates are routine.

Unlike packaged products, web-based applications can be updated seamlessly without disruption. This practice stems from the open-source movement, where anybody can improve a piece of software. Advocates of this approach suggest that, given a large enough base of beta testers, every problem can be identified and fixed. It even has its own law, known as Linus's Law, after **open-source** hero Linus Torvald.

Perpetual beta was first described by Tim O'Reilly (see **AJAX**) in 2005 as a characteristic of Web 2.0 services. Pioneering companies like Gmail and Flickr produced their platforms in the open, almost treating users as co-developers. Web 2.0 companies embrace the open-source motto, 'Release early and release often'. Facebook updates its site twice a day; Flickr releases new builds up to every 30 minutes. It makes sense. New features are introduced to select users to see how they are received, popular features are rolled out to all users, and less-favoured functionality is abandoned. The more regular the updates, the less code is thrown away.

This is clearly a huge divergence from the standard software-release cycle. Companies like Microsoft release upgrades every two or three years. This is understandable. Microsoft has more than a billion users. An unpopular change can be extremely costly. However, this approach is no longer feasible. Web 2.0 companies move in real time, and if traditional software companies wish to compete, they need to do the same. Microsoft has seen the light and has announced that it will soon switch to weekly updates.

Users are happy to accept that web services are always in beta as long as their voice is heard. There is even cachet in being part of a select beta-tester group. Part of the groundswell around Gmail was that the beta version was not available to everyone.

Perpetual beta recognizes the organic nature of the Web. As it grows, it acknowledges and responds to feedback from millions of users around the world. It is a constantly evolving ecosystem that ebbs and flows on the tide of user input. We are all beta testers now. ■

'We're all beta testers now.'

$$6x - 7i > 3(2x - 7u) = i <3 u$$

IDEA № 78
ONLINE DATING

Whether for friendship, marriage or sex, we are programmed to look for love. Before online dating, it used to be a romantic affair. Now it is an algorithm.

Eighty-one-year-old professor Wu Jieqin and his 58-year-old bride Jiang Xiaohui met online. 'The internet does not belong to the young alone', Wu Jieqin told a local newspaper.

not quite as excruciating as being snubbed in real life, and anything that minimizes humiliation is bound to catch on. Combine this with a huge pool of similar-minded people looking for love and you have a winning formula.

Instead of looking for love in your social circle, online dating enables you to search a pool of thousands – thousands of people who have conveniently let you know their interests, their personal statistics and what they are looking for in a partner. In the same way that the Web made buying an obscure book possible, it can help us find love. According to long tail theory (see **The Long Tail**), the Web provides a market for niche products. It does not get more niche than individuals.

It is now quicker and cheaper to find love than ever before. We work longer hours. We move around more. We stay single longer. Busy lives mean less time for dating. Moving around means smaller social circles. Older people go out less. Online dating offers the answer to these barriers to love.

Online dating used to be a last resort, something people turned to when they had given up on meeting someone in their day-to-day life. Now it is not only stigma-free, but also empowering. Women find it easier to make the first move. Shy people, older people and people from

Except this is not strictly true. There have always been matchmakers. There have always been blind dates. There have always been arranged marriages. Since the invention of the newspaper in the 1700s, we have had the lonely-hearts column. The Web took this to the next level.

Online dating sites worldwide are visited by hundreds of millions of people. It is estimated that one in five marriages in the US started with an online encounter. A recent survey revealed that a third of adult Germans had looked for a partner online.

The appeal of online dating is not hard to fathom. Rejection via email is

'Instead of looking for love in your social circle, online dating enables you to search a pool of thousands.'

Ashley Madison is an online dating service for people who are already in a relationship. Its slogan is 'Life is short. Have an affair.'

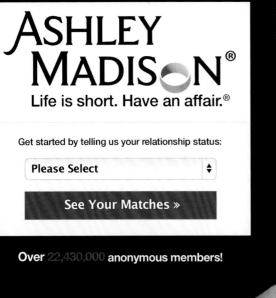

ASHLEY MADIS N®
Life is short. Have an affair.®

Get started by telling us your relationship status:

Please Select ⬍

See Your Matches »

Over 22,430,000 **anonymous members!**

minority groups can find a place to court like-minded others.

The Web has moved dating beyond time and place to shared interests. It offers a solution to people who have typically found it harder to cultivate relationships, and it fits conveniently into our busy schedules. But ultimately, it is just another way of meeting someone, indicating a deep emotional acceptance that the Web is now a normal part of life. ∎

A journey of a thousand miles begins with a single click

A reindeer captured running down a Norwegian road in 2010, one of many strange and compelling images harvested from Google Street View by Canadian artist, Jon Rafman for his ongoing project The Nine Eyes of Google Street View.

IDEA № 79

SURROGATE TRAVEL

Released in 1897, *The Haverstraw Tunnel* was a silent movie featuring a train travelling along the West Shore Railroad in New York. Filmed by a cameraman strapped to the front of the train, it was the first example of a 'phantom ride'.

In 1904, George Hale collected a number of these films and created an attraction called 'Hale's Tours of the World'. Offering trips to 'the Colonies or any part of the world (without luggage!)', he added extra realism by introducing shaking floors and sound effects. Surrogate travel had arrived. Although Morton Heilig's Sensorama machine added 3-D images, stereo sound and even smells in the 1950s, the virtual journey remained very similar for more than 70 years (see **Augmented Reality**).

This all changed in 1978. A team from MIT strapped several cameras to the roof of a jeep and drove it round the town of Aspen, taking pictures every 3 metres. The collected photos were put on a laser disc, connected to a computer and controlled by touchscreen. For the first time, the Aspen Moviemap put the viewer in charge.

In 2007, Google took the Moviemap model and scaled it up. A fleet of vehicles with roof-mounted cameras set about photographing every public street in the world. Geotagging them as they went, they took photographs every 10 metres in nine different directions. The result – Street View – is the most comprehensive photo-documentation project the world has ever seen.

Google Street View adds another layer of information to Google Maps. Dragging the pegman to a spot on the map results in an eye-level photograph of the street. Clicking in a direction starts a zoom-and-pan stop-motion animation down the street. Like any technology that becomes ubiquitous, Street View is incredible the first time you experience it, then it becomes the norm.

Street View has tremendous implications. From house buying to military training, the potential for surrogate travel is enormous. Not only can we visit places without leaving our homes, but also moments in time are being archived on a massive scale.

'The most comprehensive photo-documentation project the world has ever seen.'

Following the Japanese earthquake and subsequent tsunami in 2011, many people lost everything, including their photographs. Google Street View is the only visual record of their lives before the devastating event.

Street View has changed the way we navigate the world, but has it also changed the way we relate to it? Jon Rafman, author of *The Nine Eyes of Google Street View*, calls Street View a cultural text. Playing the role religions and ideologies have in the past, it provides a framework for our experience. In the same way that photographs become our memories, will Street View become our reality? ∎

Playing the field

CASUAL GAMING

Casual games are easy to understand and require no special skills, and players can dip in and out of them as they please. Early examples are Microsoft's Minesweeper and Solitaire, shipped with Windows. More recent examples are FarmVille and Angry Birds.

As the video games industry matured, its products became increasingly complex. Pacman gave way to Grand Theft Auto. Pong evolved into FIFA Soccer. These games required sophisticated skills and commitment to complete. They also became increasingly focused on a single audience. They were made by young men, for young men. In the process, they alienated the wider market.

With their relatively low production costs, casual games buck the trend. Game play is simple, the rules are easy to understand and they require no advanced skills. They appeal to both sexes and all age ranges.

The slow connection speeds of the 90s led to the rediscovery of early video games. The simplicity of games like Space Invaders suited the limited bandwidth of the time. Often made in Macromedia Flash, another advantage to both developers and players was that they could be played in a single sitting. Another fillip to the casual game also came in the form of a limitation – with their small screen sizes, games such as Tetris were popular on mobile phones.

The major player in the casual game space is Zynga. Its games, which include FarmVille and Mafia Wars, have added another layer to social networks. Heavily inspired by Japanese role-playing games such as Harvest Moon, Zynga launched FarmVille on Facebook in June 2009. Within six weeks, it had 10 million daily users. FarmVille alone has since earned Zynga revenues of over $1 billion.

It is the accessibility of casual games that makes them so attractive. Most of us are within arm's reach of a smartphone or a browser at all times. At the click of a mouse or the sweep of a finger we can be knee-deep in virtual fertilizer.

The mass adoption of casual games is no surprise. Whether it is a crossword, hangman or I-Spy, as long as we have had spare time, we have filled it with casual games. FarmVille and games like it are simply the digital equivalent.

FarmVille represents a breakthrough moment in the history of video games.

It signifies the mass acceptance of video games as a recreational activity. Video games are no longer the sole domain of young men. As familiar as board games and party games, the casual game can be enjoyed by the whole family. ∎

Screenshots from Zynga's FarmVille.

'As more and more platforms open their data streams, we get closer to the Semantic Web.'

The Museum of London's Street Museum app lays historical pictures of images over present-day scenes.

Greater than the sum of the parts

IDEA № 81
MASHUP

The Marauder's Map plots every inch of Hogwarts and pinpoints every person in the school, even the ghosts. In the same way as *The Daily Prophet* foresaw the iPad, the Marauder's Map is a magical realization of the mashup.

A mashup is a Web-based application that uses two or more sources to create a new, hybrid service. One of the first mashups was developed at the University of Edinburgh in 1994. The World Wide Earthquake Locator used data from the National Earthquake Center and displayed it on the Xerox PARC Map Viewer. The result was a map that plotted up-to-date earthquake information within hours of it happening.

But mashups really took off in 2005. Enterprising hackers created housingmaps.com, a site plotting room rental ads from Craigslist on Google Maps. Google saw the potential and released an Application Programming Interface (API) that allowed inventive developers to manipulate Google Maps in creative ways. A flurry of mashups followed. Historypin is a user-generated archive that invites people to pin historical photos, videos and audio recordings to Google Maps. Trendsmap.com is a global map of Twitter hashtags. Pothole Season tells you where all the potholes in Canada are and provides routes that avoid them. The Season Phenology Visualization Tool displays sightings of plants and animals across the US.

But not all mashups involve maps. Amazon, eBay, Foursquare, Flickr, Last.fm, Spotify, Twitter, Wikipedia and YouTube all provide APIs. Sonar combines Twitter, Facebook and Foursquare to alert you if your friends are nearby. The Royal Observatory combines Flickr images with Astrometry.net data to create a comprehensive photographic record of the night sky. Aaron Koblin's 'The Wilderness Downtown' uses Google Street View to create a personalized video for Arcade Fire's 'We Used to Wait'.

As more and more platforms open their data streams, we get closer to the Semantic Web envisioned by the fathers of hypertext, Vannevar Bush, Ted Nelson and Tim Berners-Lee. The potential of shared data is enormous (see **Big Data**). It can help us to predict earthquakes, map the night sky, make incredible pop videos and almost anything else we can imagine. Plotting ghosts on a map may be a way off yet, but mashing up data really can create equally magical results. ∎

Broadcast yourself

'Me at San Diego Zoo', the first video on YouTube, uploaded on 23 April 2005 by co-founder Jawed Karim.

IDEA № 82
YOUTUBE

A limitless bank of streamable songs, trailers, talks, films, best-ofs and random home videos – all for free. What's not to like? Nothing. That's why YouTube is the third most visited site on the Web.

YouTube has made stars of talking dogs, laughing babies and South Korean rappers. It's democratized TV and redefined what it means to be popular.

It began on 23 April 2005 when co-founder Jawed Karim uploaded a short clip entitled 'Me at San Diego Zoo'. At the time, finding online video was like a treasure hunt. Clips were scattered across webpages, FTP sites and peer-to-peer networking services like BitTorrent. Karim and his ex-Paypal colleagues Chad Hurley and Steve Chen sensed a gap in the market. They set out to create the Flickr of online video, where Janet Jackson's wardrobe

malfunction could be seen alongside hard news like the devastating tsunami of the same year.

Less than two years later, the video-sharing site was acquired by Google for $1.65 billion. Boosted by higher bandwidth and cheap camcorders, YouTube became a must-visit site. Equal parts entertainment, research tool and marketing channel, it revolutionized the way people used the Web. Not only could users watch endless videos of amusing cats and cute babies, but also they could learn how to wire a plug, tie a bow tie, or parachute into the middle of the Arab Spring uprisings.

'More than six billion hours of video is consumed on YouTube each month.'

Brands have also sensed a shift in attention from TV to YouTube and refocused their marketing activity accordingly. Ads for Old Spice and Evian were made first and foremost for a YouTube audience, to be enjoyed and shared in their own right. Online demonstration videos for Blendtec's 'Will it Blend?' YouTube channel did not have a TV audience in mind. Bugaboo's instructional videos stopped many new parents pulling their hair out.

'Lonelygirl15' was a made-for-YouTube TV series, and Psy's ambitions went way beyond the boundaries of the Korean Central Television network. In fact, 'Gangnam Style' attracted the attention of world leaders. UN Secretary-General Ban Ki-moon called the song a 'force for world peace'.

World peace may be stretching it, but YouTube has certainly been responsible for breaking down national and cultural borders. The flow of popular culture is no longer one directional from English-speaking countries to other parts of the globe.

In April 2011 YouTube Live was launched, covering anything from the presidential elections to Felix Baumgartner's skydive from the edge of space. Whether the content comes from a user, a citizen journalist or a brand, YouTube is beating TV at its own game. ∎

The Guggenheim Foundation initiative YouTube Play allows video artists to upload works to YouTube for possible exhibition at Guggenheim museums.

Uncensored and immediate news

MICROBLOGGING

There have been Tweets from parliament, the Vatican, space and the womb. It has caused governments to fall and society to change. And it was all put together in two weeks in 2006 by a bunch of people who should have been doing something else.

While other kids were interested in trains and Lego, Jack Dorsey was interested in how cities worked. In particular, he loved couriers. So much so that in 1992, at the age of 16, he started a bicycle messenger service of his own: 'I put my brother and me on bikes, just so I could write the dispatch software.' He quickly found out that St. Louis had no need for bicycle couriers, but the software he created is still used by courier companies today.

In 1997, during the second year of an engineering degree in Missouri, Dorsey came across a New York City-based company called Dispatch Management Services, which managed dispatch centres for couriers. Two weeks later he had moved to New York and was writing software for them. It was his dream job. 'We had couriers on CB radios, on PDAs and on cell phones. We had taxis and emergency vehicles with GPS. They're all reporting constantly where they are and what work they're doing and it's all flowing into this one system that a dispatcher can view in real time on a map. That's what's going on in the city! I wanted that same thing for my friends.'

Dorsey was a keen user of instant messaging, which he loved, but it was tied to his desktop computer. One

Jack Dorsey, founder of Twitter.

sleepless night he created a program that allowed him to send updates from his RIM 850, one of the first two-way pagers. The idea for Twitter had been born.

After a brief period running his own software company, training as a massage therapist and pursuing a career in botanical illustration, Dorsey decided to get back into programming. He joined Odeo, a podcasting company set up by Evan Williams, who had launched Blogger, the first blog platform (see **Blogging**). One of Dorsey's co-workers introduced him to SMS and he saw that it was a perfect platform for his updates program. SMS would restrict his service to 160 characters – 140 if you reserved 20 for the user address, but so what? Status updates were short and punchy anyway.

Dorsey and his team set to work on a prototype and two weeks later, on 21 March 2006, Dorsey sent the first Tweet, 'inviting coworkers'. The understated request was reminiscent of Alexander Graham Bell's first telephone call 130 years earlier: 'Mr. Watson, come here, I want you.' Like the telephone, the impact of Twitter would be enormous. Not that everybody recognized it at the time.

TechCrunch reviewed the service in July that year. Some of the comments make great reading, one post reads, 'I think this is the dumbest thing ever! Who would want all their personal text messages on a public website for anyone to read and track?' Good question, Justin. About a billion of us, since you ask. Despite some initial scepticism, the service began to catch on, and in 2007 Twitter span out of Odeo as a separate company, with Dorsey at the helm.

There are now half a billion Tweets a day, ranging from the inane to the profound. What they all share is their intrinsically democratic nature. They are uncensored and immediate. From the Arab Spring to the reporting of ice on Mars, Twitter has fundamentally changed the way in which we create and consume news. ∎

Pope Benedict's first Tweet, on 12 December 2012.

'Despite its success in Japan, the QR code has not caught on as well in the rest of the world.'

A still from the video for the Pet Shop Boys single 'Integral' created by the Rumpus Room. QR codes were embedded throughout, linking to online content related to civil liberties.

Quick response or no response?

IDEA № 84
THE QR CODE

On 26 June 1974, at Marsh's Supermarket in Ohio, cashier Sharon Buchanan scanned the world's first barcode. The product was a ten-pack of Wrigley's Juicy Fruit. The price, 67 cents.

The barcode would stay in its one-dimensional format for 20 years. This all changed in the early '90s at Denso Wave, a subsidiary of Toyota. An engineer called Masahiro Hara was tasked with creating a barcode that could hold more information than the existing format. His solution was the Quick Response (QR) code – a barcode that could be read horizontally and vertically.

Traditional barcodes are scanned by a beam of light. Hara's version could not only hold more information but also be read digitally. The biggest challenge, however, was how to scan this more complex code accurately. Hara's solution was to add positional information. The reader first locates three distinctive squares at the corners of the QR code and then normalizes the image. The rest of the black squares throughout the QR code carry the data.

In 1994, Toyota employed Hara's QR code to identify and track parts throughout its manufacturing process. Generously, the company chose not to enforce its patent, and QR codes were soon adopted across Japanese industry.

For eight years, the QR code remained an industrial tool. Then, in the early 2000s, in order to make their production processes more transparent, these codes were made available to the public. Handset manufacturers built QR code-readers into smartphones; NTT DoCoMo, a Japanese telecoms company, ran advertising campaigns teaching people how to use them.

The advertising industry was quick to see the codes' potential. Supermarkets began them as mobile coupons. Food producers used them to provide additional nutritional information. The film industry added them to posters so people could watch trailers on their phones. Many other businesses simply embedded URLs into QR codes so people could visit their website without having to type in an address.

Despite its success in Japan, the QR code has not caught on as well in the rest of the world. There was a flurry of excitement in 2007, with the release of the iPhone, but the QR code has not lived up to the hype. This is partly a matter of timing. Advancements in image-recognition technology and augmented-reality applications have increased expectations beyond a glorified barcode. Crucially, though, there is widespread confusion about how they work. People expect to be able to point their camera phone at a QR code and immediately get an enhanced experience. Finding and installing the appropriate app is proving a step too far, especially when the result is often just a link to a corporate website. ∎

News from the people formerly known as the audience

IDEA № 85

REAL-TIME REPORTING

The first time many people heard of the brutal murder of British Army soldier Lee Rigby by two Islamic extremists in May 2013 was via Twitter. Many more people then watched a shaky video of one of the suspected killers covered in blood and holding a meat cleaver.

The video was shot on a phone. Another man, out shopping, live-Tweeted the killing. Professional journalists soon descended on the scene, but their role was to fill in the blanks rather than document the event.

The ubiquity of technology means that ordinary people can report breaking news faster than traditional media reporters. Social networking and the mobile phone have propelled citizen journalism to the front line of news reporting. Initially some journalists feared that unregulated, low-quality citizen reporting will jeopardize their profession; Morley Safer, a CBS correspondent, went as far as saying 'I would trust citizen journalism as much as I would trust citizen surgery.'

Some of the criticism is valid. CNN, the *New York Post* and others, for example, ran headlines about the Boston marathon bombing gleaned from Twitter that later proved false. By and large, though, citizen journalists have emerged as promoters of human rights and democratic values. Notable examples of street reporting are the Arab Spring and Occupy Wall Street.

Increasingly, ordinary people are influencing the mainstream news agenda. CNN's iReport has over a million contributors, and in the UK *The Guardian* has recently launched Guardian Witness, specifically for footage shot on mobile phones. In South Korea, OhmyNews is a prominent news site, populated by ordinary people. With the motto 'Every Citizen is a Reporter', it has been credited with transforming South Korea's political environment.

Professional journalism is alive and well. A symbiotic relationship has developed between professional and citizen journalists. Tweets, photographs and videos captured by ordinary people, as events unfold, do not replace traditional reporting: they enhance it. Ordinary people supply the source material, and in return the mainstream media reflects their views. Soon we will just call it journalism.

'Increasingly, ordinary people are influencing the mainstream news agenda.'

'The Mobile Web has transformed not only how we browse the Web but also how we live our lives.'

Pocket power

THE MOBILE WEB

By the end of 2014, there will be more mobile devices than people on earth. Most of them will have WiFi connectivity. Wherever we go, we are connected.

The Nokia 9500 Communicator, introduced in 2004, was the first phone able to render HTML pages.

The first WiFi-enabled mobile phones appeared in Japan on the NTT DoCoMo network in 1999. At the time, Europe and the US were using Wireless Application Protocol (WAP), a standard made specifically for mobile devices. It is fair to say that it never really caught on. Not only were connection speeds poor, the content was too. The first WiFi-enabled phone in the US and Europe appeared in 2004. With its QWERTY keyboard and Microsoft-compatible software, the Nokia 9500 Communicator was popular with business users but failed to excite consumers. By this time the number of people in Japan accessing the Web via mobile phone exceeded the number browsing on a PC.

The launch of the iPhone in 2007 was pivotal. Before the iPhone, smartphones were first and foremost phones. Apple flipped this on its head. The iPhone is a hand-held entertainment system that you can make calls on. Key to its success was the best mobile Web-browsing experience the world had ever seen. This was largely thanks to the touchscreen interface and its pinch-and-zoom functionality. A webpage designed for a PC could now be viewed reasonably well on a phone.

Google recognized the paradigm shift, releasing its Android operating system in 2008. Other phone manufacturers followed as quickly as they could. Touchscreen interfaces, larger screens and faster connections made the Web truly mobile. Adoption rates soared.

Exploring the Web from our phone adds another dimension to our browsing experience. Mobile maps mean we never have to ask for directions again. Location-based search makes it easier to find a local retailer, taxi or cash point. **Augmented reality** enables a whole host of other services.

For more than 30 years, the PC dominated computing. The post-PC era, ushered in by the iPhone, is driven by the mobile Web. We now work, play, shop, organize and socialize on the move.

As more and more devices connect to **the cloud**, our smartphone becomes more central. Not only is it our primary communication tool, but also it is a hand-held computer and personal entertainment system. It will become our virtual identity. No wonder we get anxious when we leave it in the back of a cab. ■

If you want something done, do it yourself

IDEA № 87

USER-GENERATED CONTENT

Ever since there has been content, there has been user-generated content (UGC). In fact, it only became user-generated when it had an opposite – professionally made content produced for broadcast.

In this context, UGC's earliest form is 'letters to the editor'. But as these are often aligned with a particular publication's tone and politics, they have little in common with UGC as we now understand it. User-generated content today has an anarchic quality. An extension of the DIY ethic of punk culture, its roots are in fanzines, mix tapes and pirate radio, a reaction against the mass-media machine.

The roots of the Web lie in this DIY culture. Its precursor, **bulletin boards**, was created by individuals for individuals. There was no commercial return, no editorial policy and little censorship. Anybody could say anything. As the Web took hold, this attitude pervaded the forums and chat rooms that were the mainstay of the early Web.

The mid-'90s saw the commercialization of the Web. Brands and broadcasters impressed their traditional, one-way communication models on this new medium. For a while they were successful, but this was not sustainable. The dot-com companies that survived the crash understood this – they had UGC at their heart. Amazon's point of difference is its customer reviews; eBay is built on a peer-to-peer market; Google depends on user-generated links; Wikipedia is entirely written and edited by its users; even Google depends on user-generated links.

The advent of blogs was a tipping point. Users had taken back control of their space. The first **blogging** platform, Open Diary, launched in 1998 with the slogan 'Read Life. Write Life'. It signalled the start of the social-media revolution.

Blogs started the revolution, but it was fuelled by the consumer electronics industry. Digital cameras and smartphones provided a means for self-expression never before available. New platforms, like Myspace, Facebook, Flickr and YouTube, emerged to help us to connect and share this content. We have not looked back.

User-generated content is at the heart of the Web – a reaction against 100 years of passive media consumption. Whenever we participate in something, we increase our understanding of it. This is the true value of UGC. Rather than let the world wash over us, we play an active role in shaping it. ∎

A selection of user-created frames from Aaron Koblin and Chris Milk's 'Johnny Cash Project'. The user-generated video evolves as more people participate.

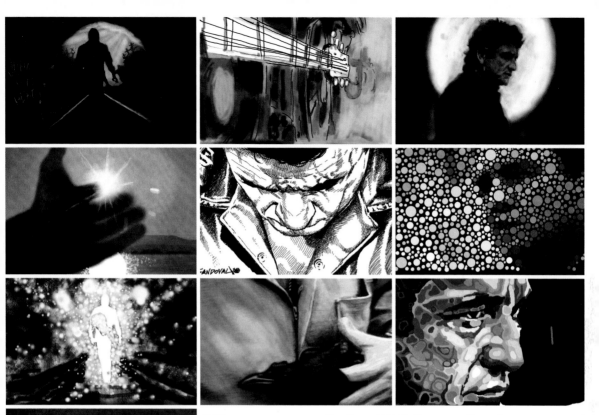

'Blogs started the UGC revolution, but it was fuelled by the consumer electronics industry.'

'Tech tapeworms in the intestines of the internet'

IDEA № 88

AGGREGATION

It is not news that we no longer get our news from newspapers. From news and reviews to classified information, aggregation sites now provide us with the stories that are most interesting to us.

Flipboard presents socially aggregated content in a magazine format.

Content aggregators gather stories from across the Web to share in a single, convenient place. With billions of webpages competing for our attention, aggregation has become an essential way of filtering out the noise. Rather than having to wade through pages of irrelevant content, you can choose a voice you trust and have content curated for you.

Sites like the Drudge Report, Fark, the Huffington Post, Reddit and Google News are all examples of news aggregation sites. Launched in 1997, the Drudge Report consists mainly of links to stories sourced from mainstream media in the US. Each link carries a headline written by Matt Drudge or his editors. (The Drudge Report rose to fame in 1998 when it broke the Monica Lewinsky story before other traditional media outlets; see **The Drudge Report**.) Fark is more irreverent. Drew Curtis launched the site in 1999 as a way to share news stories with his friends. The first article he posted was about a fighter pilot who had crashed while attempting

to moon another pilot. In 2005 the Pulitzer Prize-winning Huffington Post launched as a liberal alternative to the Drudge Report. As well as aggregated content, the Post features original stories from journalists and celebrities.

While the Drudge, Fark and the HuffPo all have editors sifting through content to choose the stories their readers are most likely to enjoy, an editor is not always essential. Social news site Reddit is entirely crowd-sourced. Users submit links and other users vote the story up or down. Google News disposes with the human touch altogether, using an algorithm to select the most relevant stories.

Aggregation sites do not just have to be used for news. Rotten Tomatoes gathers all film reviews into a single place. WikiLeaks infamously does the same for classified information. Similar sites exist for music, financial services, cars, cameras ... the list goes on. More recent aggregation services collate news from the social web. Flipboard collects content from social networks

i feel invisible to you

i feel that there is nothing i can really do but wait

i feel in love with carolyn

i feel fine when i see this

i love how i feel today

i feel so much of my dad alive in me that there isn't even room for me

i feel like i'm insane or something

i know you are watching out over me from up there i can't help but feel selfish and wish you were down here with me

i feel these weirdos are actually an asset to college life

and other feeds, presenting it in magazine format that users can 'flip' through.

This is not without controversy. Newspapers constantly complain about aggregators stealing their content. Robert Thompson, editor of the *Wall Street Journal*, does not mince his words, calling them 'tech tapeworms in the intestines of the Internet'. This may be true, but it is not going to change. Like all mass-media companies, the WSJ is no longer a distributor of news. It is a content creator and it needs to shape its business model accordingly. ■

Jonathan Harris and Sep Kamvar's We Feel Fine *searches the Web for occurrences of the phrase 'I feel' and then categorizes these feelings by age, gender and location. Through millions of individual stories, the site becomes 'a barometer for the world's emotions'.*

App app and away

THE APP STORE

In January 2011, the American Dialect Society presented its 2010 'Word of the Year' award to an abbreviation. The 'app' had become part of everyday language.

Angry Birds is one of the most successful apps of all time. Every day, users spend 200 million minutes playing the game.

There would be no App Store without iTunes. By creating a benchmark music player and a dedicated platform for downloading music, Apple changed the music industry. Not only did iTunes spell the end of the CD, it also tackled online piracy. The CEO of Sony Music, Doug Morris, sums it up: 'Steve [Jobs] created something that made it so easy for people to buy music. He had a complete thought that went from iTunes to the iPod. It made complete sense and it was something he felt people would be willing to pay for. In the end, he was right. It was all about having the right product.'

But Jobs knew the iPod would not be the right product for very long. Sooner or later, mobile phones and MP3 players would converge. The iPod was on borrowed time. In June 2007, Apple launched the iPhone. Its touchscreen interface was revolutionary, but it was not just Jonathan Ive's elegant design

that made it so desirable. Thanks to the app, the iconic phone was hardly a phone at all, it was a hand-held computer.

In 2008, replicating its winning formula, Apple launched the App Store, a dedicated platform that allows users to browse and download Apple-approved apps. It was an immediate success. When the iPhone was first released, there were 500 apps on offer. Within a year, thanks to third-party developers, there were 55,000.

Apps meant that the iPhone could be a browser, a route-planner, an entertainment system, a photo-editor, a torch, a piano or just about anything else – and often for free.

Competitors launched similar platforms, including Google Play, the Amazon Appstore and Blackberry App World. Despite Apple's best efforts, the term 'app store' is now generic, referring to any platform that allows self-contained programs to be downloaded to mobile devices.

By January 2013, the App Store had topped 40 billion downloads. Within five years, it has totally transformed the **mobile Web**. Web users in transit can get the rich experience they have become used to, without the wait. Thanks to the app, the mobile Web is no longer a stripped-down version of the desktop equivalent. Quite the opposite: it is enhanced. ∎

A mosaic of apps made by taptaptap.
com in December 2008 to celebrate
10,000 apps in the App Store.

People power

IDEA № 90
CROWDSOURCING

In 1996, photographer Rick Smolan reinvented the time capsule. He invited writers, photographers, designers and computer programmers from across the world to collaborate on a photo essay, '24 Hours in Cyberspace'.

Depicting the impact of the Web on the everyday lives of different people around the world, the project had 4 million hits in the 24 hours it was active. It was the largest one-day collaborative online event of its time.

Although it was almost a decade before the term came into public use, '24 Hours in Cyberspace' was one of the earliest examples of online 'crowdsourcing', the term coined in 2005 by Jeff Howe and Mark Robinson of WIRED magazine to describe the emerging practice of distributing labour-intensive tasks across online users and communities – in other words, 'the crowd'.

The open-source movement has been harvesting the collective power of individual programmers since the 60s. What is true of the programming community seems to be true of people in general. While the benefit is sometimes monetary, more often contributors are motivated by kudos, altruism and even good old-fashioned problem-solving.

Crowdsourcing works on the basis that 'the wisdom of the crowd' is greater than that of an individual, even if that individual is an expert – an idea James Surowiecki devoted a whole book to.

Surowiecki's opening example in *The Wisdom of Crowds* dates back to 1906, when the crowd at a county fair were asked to guess individually the weight of a butchered ox. The average guess was much closer than that of cattle experts.

Just as we have moved on from the days of butchered oxen, so the wisdom of the crowd has been harnessed in ever more innovative ways. In the aftermath of 2005's Hurricane Katrina, thousands of volunteers worked together to create the Katrina PeopleFinder Project, an online database of those missing and found, and a virtual-messaging centre for those trying to locate family and friends.

Crowdsourcing has been used to solve programming problems, translate books, create logos, produce interactive maps and find cures to diseases. Kickstarter uses the crowdsourcing approach as an alternative form of financing start-up businesses. Dell IdeaStorm uses the collective power of its customers to come up with new ideas for products and services. The list goes on. Forget too many cooks, this is all about people power. ∎

186

‘Crowdsourcing works on the principle that "the wisdom of the crowd" is greater than that of an individual’

Playground psychology

GAMIFICATION

More than 5,000 years ago the ancient Egyptians played a board game called Senet. The object was to race your opponent along an S-shaped path to the final square of a rectangular board. Winners could look forward to a glorious afterlife. Losers had better keep practising.

Board games were a favourite pastime in ancient Egypt. Senet was played by two people, either on a board, like the one found in Tutankhamen's tomb, or simply scratched into the earth.

The outcomes of today's games are not quite as important, but whether they are played on a park, on a board or online, the fundamental motivation remains the same: self-betterment.

All games share a set of common attributes – rules, interaction, scoring and an element of surprise. It turns out that these characteristics are perfectly suited to the Web.

By definition, computerized environments are rules-based and websites are inherently interactive. Friends, followers, likes and shares are all indicators of performance. Add to this irregular rewards at irregular intervals and we introduce the perfect incentive. If a pigeon is rewarded with a seed every time it pecks a lever, it will repeat the task when it is hungry, but if it is only rewarded intermittently, it will peck the lever continually. The same is true when we visit a social networking site. Until we get there, we do not know if someone will have liked our post, shared a link or updated their status. It is this unpredictability within a predictable system that drives our engagement.

Our love of games has not escaped the notice of marketers. By giving away useful tools, brands can earn our time and attention. When done well, these are more than marketing gimmicks. They embed a brand into people's daily lives. The Nike+ running app is the most obvious example. The combined app,

'Games are not just about winning, but they are not just about taking part either.'

website and bracelet tracks performance against goals and shares results with the Nike+ community. Similarly, Fiat's eco:Drive assesses your driving skills, while LinkedIn incentivizes you to keep your CV up to date.

Games are not just about winning, but they are not just about taking part either. They are about improving. Central to enjoying games, social networking sites and branded utilities is feedback. By providing feedback, we learn how to master tools. By mastering

the tools, we gain a feeling of achievement and the respect of our peers. Fundamentally, playing games and improving our skills raises self-esteem. All people play games. No wonder – they make us happy. ■

The Apple and Nike collaboration Nike+ measures and records the distance and pace of a run and uploads it to the user's personal dashboard.

Closed encounters
of the Facebook kind

IDEA № 92

OPEN ARCHITECTURE

The Web was built on open standards. HTML, HTTP and URLs can all be used without permission or payment. As a result, it has become the most powerful resource the world has ever seen.

Universal Serial Bus (USB) is an open standard for the connection of computer peripherals to personal computers.

The primary principle underlying the success of the Web is universality. Anyone can make a webpage. Any content can be put on a webpage. Any webpage can link to any other. A webpage can be viewed at any screen size and any connection speed from any device connected to the internet. Anybody can access the Web from anywhere.

This universal accessibility is under threat. Facebook, LinkedIn and other social networks do not want to share. They capture a huge amount of personal information – your name, age, gender, location, professions, skills, friends, likes and dislikes – but they keep it to themselves. Similarly, Apple's iTunes store requires proprietary software to access it. You cannot access it from a browser, you cannot link to it and search engines cannot index it. This is a worrying trend. It goes against everything the Web stands for, everything that makes it the most widely adopted technology on the planet. As Tim Berners-Lee stated, 'The decision to make the Web an open system was necessary for it to be universal. You can't propose that something be a universal space and at the same time keep control of it.' If the

next stage of the Web – the **Semantic Web** – is ever to be fully realized, an open system is essential. Today's Web is the most efficient tool ever made for publishing and distributing documents. Tomorrow's Web will analyse and understand the data within documents. Without open standards, however, the ability to analyse big data harvested from across the Web is compromised.

Closed networks result in silos of data, and restricted and reduced innovation. As we all pay homage to the closed networks of Facebook, Apple and the Kindle, we erode the Web's fundamental principle. If we are to fulfil the potential of the Web, open standards and data portability are essential. Without them it will become the iWeb, and only one company wants that. ■

'If the next stage of the Web is ever to be fully realized, an open system is essential.'

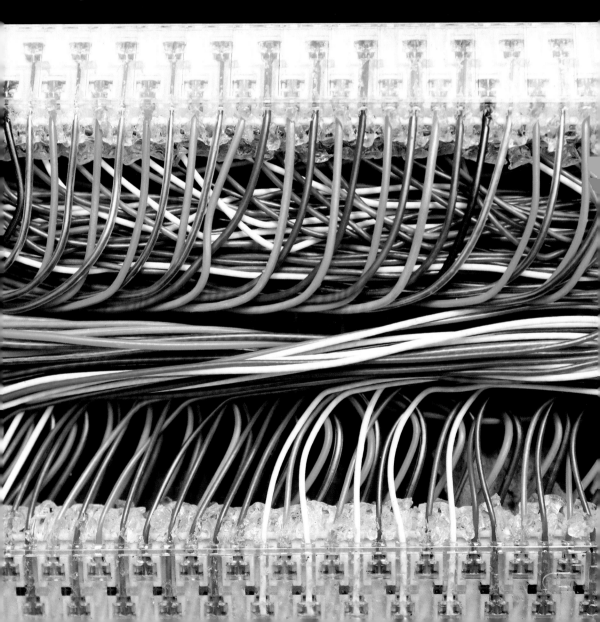

Before open standards were adopted for electrical wiring in the 1880s, many conflicting standards existed for wire sizes, colour coding and other design rules.

Aram Bartholl's work applies digital conventions to the physical world, highlighting the blurred boundary between the two.

'As phones became smart, the potential of geolocation became apparent.'

Right here, right now

IDEA № 93
GEOLOCATION

It is hard to imagine now but there was a time when we could access the Web with relative anonymity. It was a place simply to search, rather than to be found.

This all changed around 2005 when curious fellows like Tim Hibbard began to experiment with Global Positioning System (GPS) technology. Hibbard carried around a GPS-enabled phone, allowing people to track him in real time on his website, wherestim.com. Geolocation, the ability to pinpoint a person's location using their computer's IP address or GPS-enabled device, was emerging.

As phones became smart, the potential of geolocation became apparent. From tracking parcels and finding directions to localized content and offers, websites suddenly knew not only who you were but where you were.

Companies are tapping into this in different ways. Google associates search terms with locations, with astounding results. By plotting the locations in which flu symptoms appear as keywords, Google predicts influenza outbreaks faster and more accurately than the World Health Organization. Apple and Nike combine to allow fitness fanatics to track and share their runs. Ushahidi coordinates disaster relief by **crowdsourcing** information sent via mobile phone.

The social network Foursquare is at the cutting edge of geosocial services. They have turned the physical world into a game space, encouraging people to 'check in' at various locations by awarding badges and special offers. Just been to the theatre? Foursquare will recommend places to have dinner. A sunny day? Foursquare will suggest a local beer garden. At home? Foursquare will tell you about a new cafe that has just opened up round the corner. But the value of Foursquare is not the check-ins, it is the information it collects along the way.

Foursquare's vision is to do for the physical world what Google did for the Web. It is building an index of every shop, restaurant, bar, stadium, gallery, museum and concert venue. Instead of web addresses, it has street addresses. Instead of links, it has check-ins. Instead of search terms, it has your location. Overlay your social graph and 3 billion check-ins later, its dream is becoming a reality. ■

The dating app Tinder uses GPS to help people meet potential partners in their area.

Yes We Can

THE INTERNET ELECTION

On 20 January 2009, Barack Obama was inaugurated as the 44th president of the United States. It was one of the biggest days in internet history, but not quite the biggest. That honour goes to the previous November's election night, the climax of Obama's brilliantly executed digital campaign.

Democratic presidential nominee Senator Barack Obama speaking at a campaign rally in Raleigh, North Carolina, on 29 October 2008.

The Democratic Party declared Barack Obama its nominee on 27 August 2008. His campaign raised over $650 million, totally transforming expectations for future presidential elections. Whilst that enormous pot of money played a significant role, it was Obama's mobilization of young people via the social web that ultimately made him President of the United States.

Spearheaded by 24-year-old Chris Hughes, one of the co-founders of Facebook, Obama's election campaign centred on my.barackobama.com, a social network for Democrat supporters. The campaign engaged young people by tackling the issues that were important to them, harnessing their mastery of the social web. The site provided a forum to discuss policy, but it also encouraged its 2 million members to become active campaigners. As a result, millions of calls were made on behalf of the Obama campaign via the Neighbor-to-Neighbor online phone tool, and more than 200,000 events were organized. Game mechanics encouraged greater participation, recording people's activity level on their profile. Supporters who did not want to post pamphlets or make calls were gently nudged to share content, download apps and forward text messages.

In an age when we are bombarded with messages from every direction, Obama's upfront, personable style broke through. Obama built relationships with his supporters through forums and social networks such as Facebook, MySpace, YouTube, Twitter, Flickr and Digg. Facebook accounts were created for specific groups, such as Veterans for Obama, Women for Obama and African Americans for Obama. The Obama profile on BlackPlanet generated more than 450,000 friends, and Obama also engaged Asian, Hispanic, Jewish and LGBT sites. By reaching out to people in the channels they already inhabited in a way that encouraged conversation, he created a community of supporters rallying to a cause they felt part of.

An incredible 14.5 million hours of official footage was viewed on the Barack Obama YouTube channel, but it was the unofficial content that really took off. Will.i.am's 'Yes We Can' video and Obama Girl's 'I Got a Crush on Obama' were both viral sensations. Social media means a loss of control, but Obama understood that the resulting authenticity was worth the risk.

In the same way that John F. Kennedy instinctively understood and mastered television, Barack Obama is perfectly at home on the Web. His campaign did not invent anything new,

3:26 PM - 6 Nov 12 · Details

Barack Obama @BarackObama
Four more years. pic.twitter.com/bAJE6Vom
🔲 Hide photo   ← Reply   ⇄ Retweet   ★ Favorite

Barack Obama's tweet after his re-election as US president on 7 November 2012. With 788,668 shares, at the time it was the most popular Tweet ever.

529,625
RETWEETS

179,486
FAVORITES

'As Kennedy instinctively understood television, so Obama is perfectly at home on the Web. '

but by creating a joined-up digital campaign, he demonstrated the astonishing power of the Web to organize, motivate, raise money, fight smear campaigns, get out the vote and ultimately win an election. Politics will never be the same again. ■

195

Software as a service

THE CLOUD

Cloud computing is a synonym for distributed computing over a network. It means the ability to run a program on many connected computers at the same time. Its current use originates from the stylized cloud used to depict the internet on computer network diagrams.

Like Father Christmas and the Tooth Fairy, the Cloud is a figment of our imagination. It doesn't exist. It's a useful metaphor for the internet and no more. The term became popular after Amazon introduced its Elastic Compute Cloud (EC2) service in 2006. Like most computer networks, Amazon was using only a fraction of its processing power at any one time. It could not reduce capacity – it needed enough to accommodate occasional spikes – but it could share it. It decided to offer this untapped processing power to its customers.

Amazon's EC2 service raised the profile of 'the Cloud', but distributed computing has been around as long as the computing industry itself. When mainframe computers emerged in the 1950s, they were accessed via 'dumb terminals' with no computational ability. To make more efficient use of these costly mainframes, time-sharing was popular, often across time zones. Cloud computing works in exactly the same way. Resources are shared by multiple users and allocated on demand. This maximizes computing processing time and increases efficiency. Less hardware, software, power, space and personnel are required for the same functions. Resources can be easily varied to meet fluctuating demand.

Cloud computing is not just about sharing resources and economies of scale. It is a move away from dedicated hardware to a shared model where you pay for what you use. This means that software can be accessed from anywhere. You are no longer tied to a single machine. Files can no longer be lost. Backup is automatic. Downtime is reduced. Upgrades are built in. You can focus on your business, while other people focus on theirs – providing you with software. ∎

Distributed computing has been around as long as the computer.

We don't serve your type in here

EMBEDDABLE FONTS

Graphic designers' biggest grumble about the Web has always been its poor support of typography. Only a few years ago, web designers were restricted to a limited number of web-safe fonts. This all changed with TypeKit.

The first generation of web browsers, such as Mosaic and Netscape Navigator, displayed set fonts. In 1995, Netscape introduced the <font> tag, allowing web developers to choose their own fonts. Technically, you could specify any font you wanted for your site; in practice, users had to have that font installed on their computer to view it.

The set of fonts guaranteed to be pre-installed on both Windows PCs and Apple computers became known as web-safe fonts. These included Georgia and Verdana, the first fonts designed for the screen, and staples such as Arial, Courier and Times. The number of web-safe fonts grew, but almost 20 years later, web designers were still limited to just a handful.

Workarounds, such as Scalable Inman Flash Replacement (sIFR), enabled the replacement of text with Flash-based fonts. However, these increased page-loading times and were not universally accessible, so were not widely used.

In 2009, most browsers began supporting the @font-face command, which allowed a webpage to link to a font file. Web designers celebrated. Once more, in theory, they could use any font they wished. Once more, in practice, this was not the case. Most font foundries did not allow their fonts to be freely downloaded.

A company called TypeKit saw an opportunity. It licensed thousands of fonts on a web-only basis and offered a linking license to subscribers. Its platform serves fonts quickly and consistently, dealing with the differences in how browsers handle font files. Similar services, such as Google Web Fonts, Font Squirrel and Fontdeck have now emerged. The web designer's dream had come true – they could at last use any font they wish. Just make sure it's not Comic Sans. ■

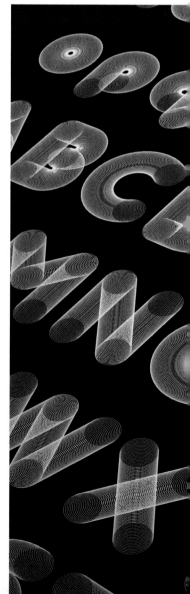

Slinky Type by Paul Hollingworth.

'The web designer's dream has come true.'

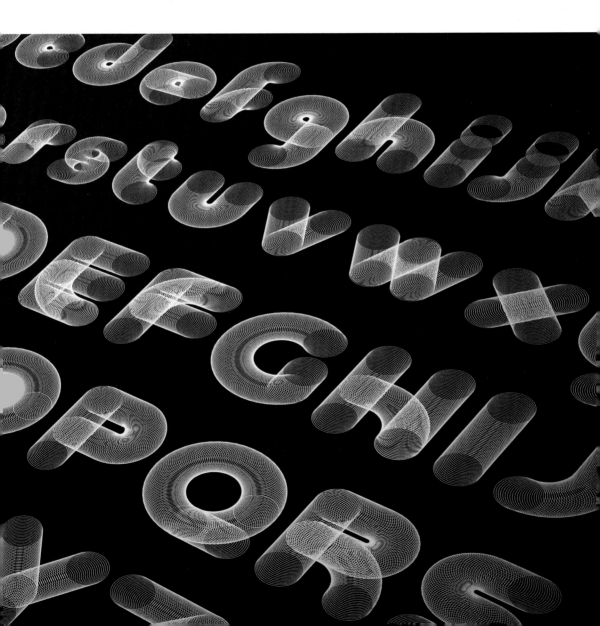

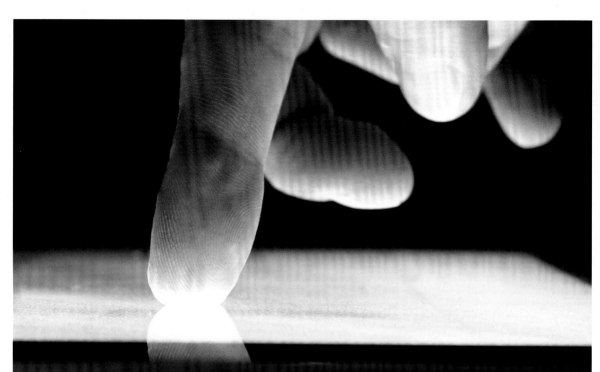

'Rather than replacing the PC, the tablet complements it.'

Touchscreen displays are inextricably linked with the success of tablet devices, challenging the 40-year dominance of the mouse.

iPad, therefore I am

IDEA Nº 97

TABLET DEVICES

When Ted Nelson described a hypermedia docuverse in 1974, he called for a user interface so simple that a beginner could understand it within ten seconds. Thirty-six years later, when Apple released the iPad, he got his wish.

When Steve Jobs announced Apple's latest revolutionary product in 2010, the touchscreen tablet PC appeared to be nothing more than a large iPhone. A large iPhone that could not be used to make calls. Why would anyone want one? Within a month, a million had been sold. Plenty of people wanted one.

The iPad is portable, good value and packed with features. More importantly, it's fun. Add thousands of apps made for the device – many available free – and you have a winning combination. Whereas computers are work tools, tablets are for entertainment.

Rather than replacing the PC, the tablet complements it. We use a conventional computer with a keyboard when we want to be productive; tablets are used from the sofa while watching TV. Perfect for email, surfing the Web, watching movies and playing games, the tablet is a lean-back, rather than a lean-forward, device.

One of the unexpected behaviours prompted by the rise of the touchscreen device is multiscreening. The TV no longer commands our full attention. While we are watching our favourite shows, we are also using our tablets to chat with friends, play games or write emails. We may start watching a film on TV in the lounge and finish watching it on a tablet in bed.

The tablet PC is no passing fad: 200 million iPads have been sold, and similar

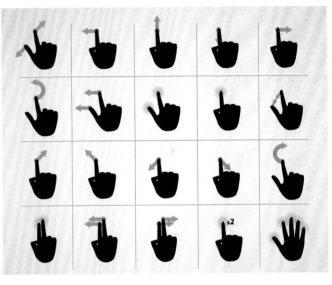

Multi-touch gestures, such as pinch and zoom, swipe and tap, have become standard across devices.

products like the Motorola Xoom and Samsung Galaxy are also proving popular. Suprisingly, it is not another hardware manufacturer that is Apple's biggest challenger. Amazon's Kindle Fire is proving yet again that it is content, not technology, that drives demand.

The iPad and its touchscreen technology is the biggest breakthrough in interface design since Douglas Engelbart introduced the mouse at the Mother of All Demos in 1968 (see **The Mouse**). The mouse was unsurpassed for 40 years. I would not bet against the tablet device having similar lasting power. ∎

One size fits all?

RESPONSIVE WEB DESIGN

We work, shop, play, socialize and relax in front of screens. We have a screen in our pocket, a screen on our desk, a screen on our lap and a screen in our front room. We use multiple screens at the same time. We move between screens to carry out tasks.

ABOVE: *Ethan Marcotte, Responsive Web Design pioneer.*

OPPOSITE: *Responsive web design makes no assumptions about a browser window's width; it responds elegantly to the device.*

increasingly the most important screen is the one on our phone. It is the last screen we look at at night. It's the one screen that cuts across our work and leisure time. Content optimized for larger screens often results in a disappointing experience on smaller screens. Cropped images, wrapped navigation, rollovers no longer working and illegible text are all common degradations. Designing for a smaller screen is equally unsatisfactory at larger resolutions. Traditionally, this has meant different layouts for each device, but with ever more screen sizes to optimize for, this is a huge task.

In a May 2010 article for A List Apart, Ethan Marcotte suggested a solution. Inspired by responsive architecture, where buildings react and adapt as people pass through them, he coined the term 'responsive web design' (RWD). In the article he states: 'Rather than tailoring disconnected designs to each of an ever-increasing number of web devices, we can treat them as facets of the same experience. We can design for an optimal viewing experience, but embed standards-based technologies into our designs to make them not only

Whether we are consuming media on a PC, a tablet device, a smartphone or the TV, we like content optimized for that particular device. This is not easy when they all have different screen sizes and interfaces and are used at different points of the day for different tasks.

Websites are traditionally optimized for desktop browsers, but

'Increasingly, the most important screen is our phone, the last screen we look at at night.'

more flexible, but more adaptive to the media that renders them. In short, we need to practice Responsive Web Design.' Responsive web design makes no assumptions about a browser window's width. It responds elegantly to the device using 'media queries', a World Wide Web Consortium standard. Navigation can be adjusted, images can be repositioned, content can be re-aligned and font sizes adjusted. It is a better experience for both the user and the developer.

Despite the hype, responsive design is just good design. Since the birth of the Web, designers have had to create webpages that worked at multiple resolutions. Screen resolutions have always varied. Just like users, they come in all shapes and sizes. It is the designer's job to accommodate them. ∎

'Thanks to the Web, we have gone from information scarcity to information overload in two decades.'

Ryoji Ikeda's Data.Tron *is part of his* Datamatic *series, a body of work that visualizes the data around us.*

The more, the merrier.
The bigger, the better

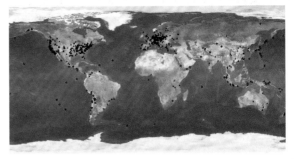

BIG DATA

The Quake-Catcher Network is the world's largest low-cost, strong-motion seismic network. It is a collaborative initiative that utilizes the sensors in internet-connected computers.

Every minute, 2 million searches are made, half a billion links are shared and 48 hours of footage are uploaded. That is a lot of data. And yet, in terms of how much is being produced worldwide, it barely scratches the surface. That is Big Data.

Big Data is the term used to describe data sets that are so large and complex that it takes a phenomenal amount of processing power to interrogate them. So why do it?

Fourteen seconds before the 2011 earthquake in Japan, every bullet train and every factory came to a halt. Many lives were saved thanks to the Quake-Catcher Network. This network is made up of thousands of laptops with free software running in the background. The software makes use of the built-in sensors designed to protect the hard drive if the laptop is dropped. If there is an earthquake, all the sensors go off at the same time. By continuously aggregating and processing the data produced by all the sensors, it is possible to brace for impact before the earthquake strikes. Fourteen seconds before, as it turns out.

In an increasingly connected world, our ability to capture and store data is staggering. We have sensors in everything, from running shoes to mobile phones. We are divulging more and more personal information to social networks. We supply more and more customer data to retailers, on-

and offline. Around 90 per cent of the data in the world today has been created in the last two years alone. Thanks to the Web, we have gone from information scarcity to information overload in two decades.

Big Data needs big computers to process it. The algorithms that crunch Big Data require thousands of servers running in parallel. Currently, only governments and web giants like Google and Amazon have the necessary resources. Barack Obama got elected off the back of it. Twice. By unifying vast commercial, political and social databases, his team was able to understand and influence individual swing voters (see **The Internet Election**). Google uses it to predict flu outbreaks, identify human trafficking hot spots and sell advertising.

When the Web was first conceived, it was intended to be more than an interconnected repository of information. The ultimate aim was the **Semantic Web**, a Web that drew meaning from information. Big Data is half the equation. ∎

When information becomes knowledge

IDEA № 100
THE SEMANTIC WEB

The dream of intelligent machines has been around almost as long as machines themselves. This dream is now becoming a reality. It is called the Semantic Web.

The term was coined by the inventor of the Web, Tim Berners-Lee: 'I have a dream for the Web ... in which computers ... become capable of analysing all the data on the Web – the content, links, and transactions between people and computers. A "Semantic Web", which makes this possible, has yet to emerge, but when it does, the day-to-day mechanisms of trade, bureaucracy and our daily lives will be handled by machines talking to machines.'

On the Semantic Web, all information exists in a format that software applications can investigate and understand. Information is automatically processed and turned into knowledge.

Knowledge is information in context. Just as today's Web marks up information so that it can be displayed, searched and indexed, the Semantic Web marks up information describing its context. By applying context to large volumes of information, new connections occur, and unexpected discoveries are made.

When information is marked up with contextual data, the information becomes more valuable. It becomes knowledge. On the Semantic Web this knowledge travels with the data. When you access a piece of information you also access the context for understanding it. Data from disparate sources is automatically merged. Vast new data sources are created from which new understanding can arise. Unstructured data becomes structured. The World Wide Web becomes a global database of knowledge.

This may sound far-fetched, but it is already happening in small pockets across the Web. Take Facebook. People and applications interact to create an ever-smarter pool of knowledge. It is learning and interpreting our behaviour. Facebook is thinking. The same is true of Amazon, eBay, Flickr, Twitter and many other websites. But as in the physical world, this knowledge is locked away in silos. By sharing this intelligence across an open network, we could take a giant step closer to realizing the Semantic Web. A Web that thinks.

A Web that thinks, a World Wide Mind, is a crazy thought. But when every piece of information in the world is linked and described, it is a logical next step. This future is not too far away. And it is not dissimilar to the vision a Belgian bibliophile had in 1935 (see **The Mundaneum**). ■

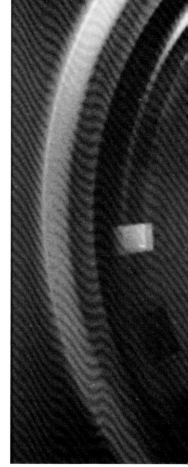

'Information with contextual data becomes more valuable.'

HAL 9000 in 2001: A Space Odyssey, *a sentient computer that can think for itself.*

Further Reading

Art

Bartholl, Aram *The Speed Book* (Gestalten, 2012)
USB sticks embedded into walls and Google Map markers positioned in public spaces are just two of Bartholl's public art installations that mashup our online and offline worlds.

Harris, Jonathan & Kamvar, Sep *We Feel Fine* (Scribner, 2009)
Constantly searching the web for new occurrences of the phrases 'I feel' and 'I am feeling' and recording the subsequent adjective, *We Feel Fine* is a barometer for the world's emotions.

Kare, Susan *Icons* (http://www.kareprints.com, 2011)
A curated look at 80 of Kare's icons created between 1983 and 2011. A zoomed-in view allows the reader to see how icons are crafted pixel by pixel.

Lialina, Olia & Espenschied, Dragan *Digital Folklore* (Merz Academie, 2009)
An homage to online amateur design and DIY culture that celebrates kittens, rainbow gradients and the animated GIF.

Rafman, Jon *The Nine Eyes of Google Street View*, 2009
Rafman's collection of strange and beautiful images accidentally captured by Google Street View.

Smolan, Rick *24hrs in Cyberspace* (Macmillan,1996)
Billed at the time as the 'largest collaborative internet event ever', it documents the impact of the internet on a single day, 8 February 1996.

Blog posts

Barlow, John Perry 'A Declaration of the Independence of Cyberspace', 1996
Barlow's declaration evokes the US Declaration of Independence and describes the internet as a borderless, stateless world where anyone, anywhere should be able to express his or her beliefs without fear of censorship. https://projects.eff.org/~barlow/Declaration-Final.html

Boulton, Jim 'Digital Archaeology', 2014
Read more about the history of the Web and the formative years of digital culture on the author's blog.http://www.digital-archaeology.org

Levin, Golan 'New Media Artworks: Prequels to Everyday Life', 2009
A list of commonplace technologies, initially conceived by new-media artists. http://www.flong.com/blog/2009/new-media-artworks-prequels-to-everyday-life/

Lialina, Olia 'One Terabyte of Kilobyteage', 2013
Screenshots automatically generated from Geocities homepages and rescued by the Archive Team in 2009.
http://oneterabyteofkilobyteage.tumblr.com

Marcotte, Ethan 'Responsive Web Design' (A List Apart article, 2010)
Marcotte suggests that rather than tailoring designs to an ever-increasing number of devices, we design them to adapt to the media that renders them. http://alistapart.com/article/responsive-web-design/

O'Reilly, Tim 'What Is Web 2.0', 2005
The post that first defined Web 2.0, describing the future of the Web as a platform. http://oreilly.com/web2/archive/what-is-web-20.html

Essays

Barbrook, Richard & Cameron, Andy 'The Californian Ideology', *Mute* magazine, 1995
Critique of West Coast neo-liberalism that raises the apparent contradiction of the freewheeling spirit of the Californian hippy movement and the entrepreneurial zeal of Silicon Valley.

Baudrillard, Jean 'Simulacra and Simulation' (Éditions Galilée, 1981; English translation, University of Michigan Press, 1994)
Essay which claims that modern society has become abstracted from reality, and that our lives have become a meaningless collection of signs and symbols. Cyberpunk takes many of its cues from Baudrillard's philosophical treatise

Bush, Vannevar 'As We May Think' *The Atlantic Magazine*, 1945
Bush's groundbreaking essay describes the Memex, a device that could store, index and connect every book and record created.

Turing, Alan 'Computing Machinery and Intelligence', 1950
Seminal essay on Artificial Intelligence that introduced the concept we now know as the Turing test.

Wells, H.G. *World Brain*, 1938
Wells' vision of a world encyclopedia based on new technologies, such as microfilm, that could be continually updated, giving the world common understanding and common purpose.

Information graphics

McCandless, David *Information is Beautiful* (HarperCollins, 2009)
Information design at its best. A visually stunning collection of infographics that make data meaningful and entertaining.

Neurath, Otto *International Picture Language*, 1936
While Director of the Social and Economic Museum, Vienna, Neurath invented information graphics as we recognize them today.

Tufte, Edward *The Visual Display of Quantitative Information*, 1982
In his first book, the pioneer of data visualization. outlines the fundamentals of information design. A modern classic.

Fiction

Borges, Jorge Luis 'The Garden of Forking Paths' (Editorial Sur, 1941; English translation *Ellery Queen's Mystery Magazine*, 1948)
A short spy story by the Argentinian master. Perhaps the earliest example of a non-linear narrative with multiple possible endings.

Clarke, Arthur C. *2001: A Space Odyssey* (Hutchinson/New American Library, 1968)
The story of Dr. David Bowman's mission to Saturn and his interactions with an artificially intelligent computer called HAL 9000.

Dick, Philip K. *Do Androids Dream of Electric Sheep?* (Doubleday, 1968)
The sci-fi novel on which *Bladerunner* is based. In a post-apocalyptic world, bio-engineered replicants are virtually indistinguishable from human beings. The empathy test used to determine the truth is a form of Turing test.

Gibson, William *Neuromancer* (Ace, 1984)
Gibson's groundbreaking debut heralded a new genre in sci-fi, recasting the computer nerd as a hard-boiled anti-hero, a cyberpunk.

Leinster, Murray 'A Logic Named Joe' (published in *Astounding Science Fiction*, 1946)
The first work of fiction to predict computers, networks and the Web.

Sterling, Bruce *Mirrorshades: The Cyberpunk Anthology*, 1986
A defining collection of cyberpunk short stories.

Reference

Berners-Lee, Tim *Weaving the Web* (HarperBusiness, 2000)
Berners-Lee reveals the Web's origins and offers his vision for the future, so that it remains a powerful force for social change and an outlet for individual creativity.

Cailliau, Robert & Gillies, James *How the Web Was Born* (Oxford University Press, 2000)
Cailliau, who with Tim Berners-Lee is the co-author of the Web, tells the story of its invention and why it was given away for free.

Cunningham, Ward & Leuf, Bo *The Wiki Way* (Addison Wesley, 2001)
The complete guide to deploying and managing a wiki.

Dawkins, Richard *The Selfish Gene* (Oxford University Press, 1976)
Dawkins suggests that human behaviours evolve in the same way as biological life. This phenomenon is defined as a meme, a unit of cultural transmission from person to person.

Drudge, Matt *The Drudge Manifesto* (NAL, 2000)
The infamous aggregator shares his opinions on politics, the media, big business and modern life.

Hoffman, Abbie *Steal This Book* (Pirate Editions/Grove Press, 1971)
A practical guide for the aspiring countercultural hippie, it exemplifies the hacker ethic and inspired a generation to challenge the status quo.

Krug, Steve *Don't Make Me Think* (2nd edition, New Riders, 2005)
The definitive book on human-computer interfaces and web usability.

Lacy, Sarah *Once You're Lucky, Twice You're Good* (Gotham, 2009)
The story of the dot-com entrepreneurs who funded Web 2.0.

Lessig, Lawrence *Free Culture* (Penguin, 2005)
How copyright law stifles progress. Released under the Creative Commons Attribution/Non-commercial licence.

Lie, Håkon Wium & Bos, Bert *Cascading Style Sheets* (2nd edition, Addison Wesley, 1999)
How and why to use CSS by the duo who created the W3C specification.

Malmsten, Ernst *Boo Hoo* (Random House, 2002)
The rise and fall of boo.com encapsulates the best and worst of the dot-com bubble.

Markoff, John *What the Dormouse Said* (Penguin, 2006)
How the '60s counterculture shaped the personal computer industry.

Marsh, Taylor *My Year in Smut* (Authorhouse, 2000)
The editor-in-chief of Danni's Hard Drive spills the beans.

Mitnick, Kevin *Ghost in the Wires* (Little, Brown, 2011)
The true story of Kevin Mitnick, possibly the most notorious hacker of all time and one-time Public Enemy Number One.

Naughton, John *A Brief History of the Future* (2nd edition, Phoenix, 2000)
Early story of the internet and where it might take us.

Negroponte, Nicholas *Being Digital* (Knopf, 1995)
The founder of MIT's Media Lab provides a history of digital media and predicts how it will evolve.

Nelson, Theodor *Computer Lib/Dream Machines*, (self-published, 1974)
A call to arms, demanding that ordinary people rise up and claim computers for themselves. Describes the unlimited potential of branching media and networked content.

Rhodes, Richard *Heddy's Folly*, 2011
The remarkable story of how film star Hedy Lamarr, star of *Samson and Delilah*, invented spread-spectrum radio, the technology that underpins WiFi.

Stephenson, Neal *In the Beginning, Was the Command Line*, 1999
A commentary on the unsustainability of the proprietary software business in the face of competition from open-source software.

Surowiecki, James *The Wisdom of Crowds*, 2005
Surowiecki's crowdsourcing manifesto suggests that large groups of people are always smarter than a small group of experts.

Wozniak, Steve *iWoz*, 2006
Describes how Wozniak invented the personal computer and had fun along the way.

Index

Picture Credits

Acknowledgements

For Miori and Kenzo.

Lots of people helped me out with this book. Peter Jones, my editor at Laurence King, and Louise Thomas, who sourced the images, both worked tirelessly. Others that I owe a debt of gratitude to are Amar Patel, Will Pike and Charlotte Thomas. Special thanks goes to Jon King, for his 'make it shorter and put more Jim in it' mantra.

I hope my family knows how much they are appreciated. I couldn't have written this book without them – or achieved much else for that matter. Thanks mum and dad for your regular trips down the A10, thanks Miori for being so supportive and thanks Kenzo for being a good sleeper.

LAURENCE KING

Published in 2014
by Laurence King Publishing Ltd
361–373 City Road
London EC1V 1LR

Tel +44 20 7841 6900
Fax +44 20 7841 6910

enquiries@laurenceking.com
www.laurenceking.com

A catalogue record for this book is available from the
British Library

ISBN 978 1 78067 370 7

Design: TwoSheds Design
Senior Editor: Peter Jones

Printed in China